Tips and Traps
for Marketing
Your Business

Tips and Traps for Marketing Your Business

Scott Cooper
Fritz Grutzner
Birk Cooper

Mc
Graw
Hill

New York   Chicago   San Francisco   Lisbon   London
Madrid   Mexico City   Milan   New Delhi   San Juan
Seoul   Singapore   Sydney   Toronto

1 2 3 4 5 6 7 8 9 0   FGR/FGR   0 9 8

ISBN 978-0-07-149489-2
MHID 0-07-149489-8

This publication is designed to provide accurate and authoritative information in regard to the subject matter covered. It is sold with the understanding that neither the author nor the publisher is engaged in rendering legal, accounting, or other professional service. If legal advice or other expert assistance is required, the services of a competent professional person should be sought.

—From a Declaration of Principles jointly adopted by a Committee of the American Bar Association and a Committee of Publishers

McGraw-Hill books are available at special quantity discounts to use as premiums and sales promotions, or for use in corporate training programs. To contact a representative please visit the Contact Us pages at www.mhprofessional.com.

Library of Congress Cataloging-in-Publication Data

Cooper, Scott W.
  Tips and traps for marketing your business / by Scott W. Cooper, Fritz P. Grutzner, and Birk P. Cooper.
    p. cm.
  ISBN 0-07-149489-8 (alk. paper)
  1. Marketing. I. Grutzner, Fritz P. II. Cooper, Birk P. III. Title.
HF5415.C588 2008
658.8–dc22
                        2007035880

This book is printed on acid-free paper.

Acknowledgments

In marketing, a great brand idea revolves around the art of sacrifice: one idea synthesized down to a powerful story. Writing a book is also the art of sacrifice—a sacrifice of time. I'd like to thank Roman Hiebing, my past co-author, for teaching me about the time and discipline it takes to write a book. Roman, your words still resound in my head, "If you can sit, you can write. It's sitting that's hard." Thanks to my wife, Liz, for making that time possible. You are simply the best. Thanks to Fritz Grutzner for making all that time enjoyable. It was fun taking our two separate stories and merging them into a more powerful one. And finally, to my son, Birk, you're the reason I decided to do this project in the first place. For you, my time is never a sacrifice.

Scott W. Cooper

The writing of a book is always both a solitary act and a team effort. The author puts the words down, but the ideas, time, and encouragement come from many sources. There are many people I would like to thank for sharing their patience and wisdom with me. My wife, Kris, played a critical role in the writing of this book, offering encouragement and good suggestions, editing the manuscript, and giving me the time to write. She makes me a better person every day. Every minute spent on this book was precious time not spent with my three girls: Eva, Sophie, and Anna. I thank them for allowing me the time to write. My marketing career has been shaped by many wise folks, but I am most indebted to Roman Paluta, Colleen Goggins, Alex Labak, and Owen Rankin. Finally, I'd like to thank Scott for the opportunity to work on this book with him. It was an enjoyable and fruitful experience.

Fritz P. Grutzner

I have been fortunate to have my Dad and Fritz as mentors. Their 50 years of combined experience have given me a great start and a solid foundation for my career. I will be forever grateful.

Birk P. Cooper

Contents

Tips and Traps for Marketing Your Business

Marketing Planning Model

Introduction: What Is Marketing?

There is only one valid definition of a business purpose: to create a customer.

—Peter Drucker

The purpose of this book is to help you plan, develop, and implement the fundamentals to successfully market your business, whether it is a billion dollar consumer goods company, a business selling to other businesses, or a small nonprofit. Every organization is unique and each one competes in a slightly different way, but the successful ones have one thing in common:

They understand what their customers really want and how to engage customers with their brand.

It sounds simple. In many ways it is simple. The format of this book is intended to keep things as simple as possible for you to effectively market your business.

Definition of Marketing

The word *marketing* gives us clues as to what the discipline is all about. A market is a group of consumers who share similar characteristics. Therefore, marketing is the discipline of:

- Identifying your target market
- Discovering the needs and wants of your target market
- Developing and executing a plan to build a relevant and differentiated offering

1

- Creating loyal customers, who have an emotional engagement with your brand

Consumers choose products and services for many reasons. If you ask them, most consumers will typically point to the functional reasons they chose a brand: the taste of the French fries, the handling of the car, or the convenience of the retailer. And yet, when it really comes down to it, there is very little functional difference between most competitive products today. How is one baby powder functionally different from another? How many consumers can really distinguish between two light beers in a blind taste test? What good marketers understand is that the feelings matter when it comes to their consumers' relationship to their brands. In a world where two products or services are nearly identical, how consumers feel about your brand can be the feather that tips the scales and makes all the difference.

TIP

Marketing is about creating a positive relationship with your target audience so that you win the ties.

Two of the top retailers in the country today, Wal-Mart and Target, are very similar on a functional level. A lot of the products these two retailers sell are similar and the prices at which they sell them are nearly identical. Both are usually found in similarly convenient locations. They both advertise heavily. And yet, when you talk to shoppers around the country, you will find very strong loyalties for one over the other. Target has generally done a brilliant job of marketing itself, while Wal-Mart is just beginning to discover their marketing shortcomings and facing significant marketing challenges. When was the last time you heard about a local group protesting the opening of a new Target? In many localities, Target is referred to by a familiar nickname: "Tarjhay." In these markets, it is not at all uncommon for a consumer to boast about purchasing a pair of shoes or a new shirt at Target. One rarely hears consumers boasting about their new Wal-Mart shoes.

Many organizations with which we have worked make the mistake of believing that marketing is solely the responsibility of the marketing department. Your customers will never see your marketing plan. They will never see your strategic plan. They will only know your company or brand from their interactions with them. Maybe they have called your customer service desk. Maybe they have tried your product. Maybe they have seen an ad. Or, perhaps, they have read an article about your president. All of these interactions help guide their feelings about your organization. The best companies understand that marketing is the responsibility of every person in the organization.

TIP

Marketing is too important to be the responsibility of just the marketing department.

When marketing becomes the company's job, you align around a target market and speak with one voice—across product, operations, and communication. When everyone in your company listens to the desires, needs, and wants of your target market, you act as one. And when these needs and wants get translated into a plan or business model that everyone follows, all of the pieces of your company act in unison. You end up consistently communicating with your customers: reinforcing who you are, what you believe in, and how you are different—whether it is in the design of your product, what your store or office looks like, your customer service policies, or how you advertise.

Tips and Traps for Using This Book

This book is organized into chapters that take you through a marketing planning process that we have found to be very useful. It also includes tips and traps that the authors have learned, sometimes the hard way, in helping organizations market their businesses. You can read every page for a detailed understanding of the process, choose just the chapters that address your specific needs, or, if you are a seasoned marketing veteran, you can skim the tips and traps in each chapter.

We have structured the book around the marketing planning model shown at the beginning of this chapter. The outside ring of the model highlights the activities necessary for any first-time business: to define the business you are in and what your brand stands for. The inner ring shows the activities most companies use to build engagement with their customers through the brand experience. We have worked at, and with, some of the largest global multinationals, as well as some of the smallest. This model is a useful tool for guiding marketing activities at any organization.

Marketing Planning Model

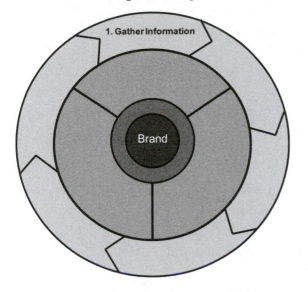

1
Gathering Information

As a general rule, the most successful man in life is the man who has the best information.
——Benjamin Disraeli

Information Good Marketers Need

We've all heard the saying, "garbage in, garbage out." It's the same when marketing your business. Understanding your market provides you with a valuable base of insights into your business, your competitors, and your customers. It will provide you with both a fact base and key insights that will drive the major tasks of choosing your target market, defining your brand, setting your objectives, and in setting strategies and tactics to make your plan happen.

TIP

Look for what you need, not what you can find. There is a swamp of information out there. Most of it is not helpful for marketing your business. The best marketers determine what they need to find before they start looking.

Here are some key pieces of information many businesses should start with:

Sales

- Size of market
- Market growth

- Market share versus key competitors over time
- Product and service usage habits

Awareness and Attitudes

- Brand awareness and shifts over time
- Brand perceptions and shifts over time

Distribution

- Industry and company channels

Pricing

- Estimated cost and pricing structure of your company and competitors
- Price elasticity of your products

Market Trends

- Current and future trends that affect demand

Competitors

- Strengths and weaknesses (product, company, distribution, pricing, communication)
- Marketing and advertising spending
- Brand positionings of key competitors
- Key competitive strategies

Culture

- Company history
- Consumer language and customs
- Company rituals

Most of the information you will need is publicly available. This may seem surprising to you, if you don't purchase expensive market share data from a provider. For most companies, a walk through the store, a studied look at the marketing of your competitors, a read through your competitors' annual reports, a Google search, and studying trade journals, along with industry articles in business publications, will offer a pretty good foundation for understanding key issues in the market.

Let's say you have a new brand of bottled water you want to market. A visit to the shelf of Wal-Mart can tell you a lot. You can roughly estimate market share from the product facings on the shelf. You can see what size assortment consumers are purchasing and what pricing strategies they are using. You can see which new products are being launched as a clue to where the category may be going. Simply observing how consumers are shopping the category can be enlightening. Do they stand in front of the aisle for minutes studying the category, or do they go right for the brand they want and leave? Good marketers spend a lot of time studying the environment in which their customers choose and use their products and services. Toyota's product development engineers spent years observing the behaviors of truck owners before successfully entering this large segment with their Toyota Tundra.

It's a good idea to provide comparison points. Single numbers often don't provide enough useful information. Reporting that you have 13 percent market share doesn't really tell your organization much at all. However, reporting that over the past three years, market share has increased from 9 to 15 percent and that your company is now third in market share, with the leader holding 47 percent and the second place competitor at 15 percent, provides important context. It shows you are gaining share in a market that is dominated by one strong competitor. It would signal that your company is probably seen as more of a niche player and that you are probably competing not as much against the leader but the other smaller players by providing a different set of benefits than the market leader. Thus, it is important to understand how consumers see your product versus the leader and the other smaller players with whom you compete. The comparison of reference points allows this insight. When you are gathering information in this section, think about the following ways to show points of comparison:

- *Compare trends within your company.* For example, growth in sales over a five-year period, increases in average sales per transaction from year to year, the use of different distribution channels over time, and the increase or decrease over time of your advertising-to-sales ratio.

- *Compare your company to the industry.* A good measure of where you are is to compare key metrics for your company to that of the industry as a whole. The industry represents the sum of your competitors. Comparing your company to the industry along key metrics provides you a snapshot of how you are doing relative to the average performance of all your competitors.

- *Compare your company to key competitors.* It's also very helpful to compare your company to the group of competitors that you've identified as your core competitive set. Many of you are in industries that have many different levels of competitors. In retail, for example, the industry is often made up of the big-box mass merchants, the mid-tier that can be found in strip centers offering value to its customers, and the specialty shops often found in malls carrying more upscale products. It helps to define the three to four competitors that most affect your success.

TIP

Keep a notebook of ideas while gathering information. Planning is not linear. Great ideas occur while you are delving into your industry, into competitive and company trends, and while exploring the insights into the target market.

We have always found that there is a time when we are first exploring a category when we have lots of ideas about what marketing strategies might work. As we learn more about the category, we discover that most of these won't work. However, the newcomer to the category looks at it with fresh eyes and often recognizes patterns of opportunity that industry insiders have dismissed long ago or overlooked. This is why we suggest that you write all your fresh ideas down. Some of them may be brilliant, but you won't know until you have finished your analysis of the data.

Additionally, as you learn more about your category and the insights of your customers relating to your company, you will often be struck by ideas on how to apply these insights. Capture these. Some of the best ideas come at the moment of understanding.

TRAP

Avoid analysis paralysis. You can never get all the background information you would like to have. Prioritize the most important information, find it, summarize it objectively, and move on.

The purpose of gathering information is to provide insights that support marketing decisions you will make. Collect enough information so that you can look at the data and understand directionally what it's telling you. For example, in most cases it's enough to understand the sales trends of the key competitors that dominate your market, without taking the time to analyze every competitor. Likewise, you can't fully understand consumers' perceptions of your business. You can get insights through observation, talking with customers and noncustomers, and doing formal market research. But in the end, you'll need to form educated opinions of the "whys" behind what you think you're hearing. At some point, you simply need to say you've learned all you're going to until you decide on a strategy and test some ideas and programs in the marketplace.

Try to remain objective as you gather information. Don't turn this activity into a marketing plan. Stay away from stating objectives or writing strategies and tactics. As you gather information, stay neutral, state the facts, and objectively summarize key findings. Remember, the purpose of gathering information is to gain an understanding of how to best market your business. You shouldn't form any conclusions at this point.

Analyzing Sales Information of Your Products and Services

Your company's sales provide a wealth of information. A review of the past five to seven years provides a perspective over time and allows you to project which products stand the best chance for growth in the future. A careful sales analysis will provide you with insights into competitive strengths, consumer demand, the success of new products and programs, and give you the basis for projecting success going forward.

TRAP

Don't just look at today. Explore the past to see the future.

Don't just look at this year's or last year's sales. The long-term picture of sales provides you with the best insights into shifts and changes and provides insights into future trends. Sometimes, the key to a brand's success happened early on in its history. Maybe the key was penetrating a new distribution channel. Maybe it was a certain advertising campaign that ran years ago. Trying to understand the long-term historical sales trends of your brand can sometimes offer a gold mine of insights for your current strategy.

For every established brand or company, there was once a time when it was getting started and sales were minimal. Most companies had a breakthrough at some point, when sales really started to take off. What about your product or service drove this rapid increase? Was it launching a new service program, innovations to your product, or launching a successful new product line? This can provide important clues about the past core foundation of your business success.

The secret of a company's current success is often waiting to be discovered somewhere in its past growth history.

TRAP

Don't ignore the parts while looking at the whole. Gather sales information for your company but also for each of your key product lines.

Your company may have many products or product categories. If that's the case, you should track sales over time for each product or product category and for the company as whole. Don't just track sales. Include a profit and market share picture as well. Consider the following:

- Sales
- Gross margin dollars (sales less cost of goods)
- Operating profit (sales less cost of goods and expenses)
- Market share versus competitors (sales as a percent of total industry sales)

Remember to track your sales relative to key competitors and relative to your industry or marketplace. Knowing you gained 3 percent in sales, the industry as a whole gained 5 percent, and the industry leader gained 12 percent provides a relative measure of performance. In this scenario, you've actually lost market share and there's a clear market leader that is capturing consumer preference.

TIP

Almost every business has a portfolio of brands or products. If that portfolio isn't managed over time, resources are very often undercommitted to the best products and overcommitted to those products that don't have a rosy future or aren't as profitable.

By examining the sales growth and relative importance of your complete product line, you establish a consistent way to continually manage your product portfolio. Years ago, the Boston Consulting group developed a matrix for looking at a product portfolio, called the BCG growth-share matrix, which is still very useful today (see Figure 1.1). Their matrix places products along two axes: market growth rate and relative market share. If you have a product with dominant market share in a high-growth market, it is one of your *stars* and it should be well supported. On the other hand, products with a weak share of market in a low-growth market are called your *dogs* and should be divested. The *question marks* are the products with a small share in a growing category. These should be watched carefully and evaluated with respect to the opportunities to grow share. The *cash cows* are the

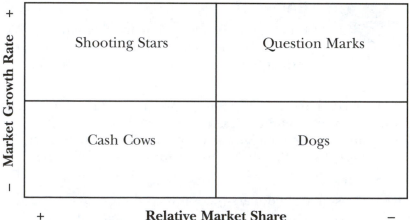

Figure 1.1. Boston Consulting Group growth-share matrix.

products in a slow-growth market that have a large market share. Cash cows are typically "milked" for cash.

TIP

The holy grail of every for-profit business is to generate profitable growth; therefore, it's important to try to discover the profit pools in your business.

As you manage your product portfolio, don't forget about tracking the profitability of your products. Successful companies place additional resources against products with the most company profitability. U-Haul had a very successful overall business. While they did not derive much profit from their truck rentals, they made a bundle on the sales of boxes and moving incidentals. Feed and grow the areas of your business that matter most.

For long-term sustainability, your profitability will need to be comparable with your competitors'. If your key competitors and the industry have higher gross margins or operating profits, determine what you need to do to bring profitability more in line with the industry.

Combine profitability insights with top-line sales insights. Success for most businesses comes from managing a smart combination of both top-line sales and profitability. If you manage only for sales growth, you could still end up losing money. If you manage only for profitability, you could starve your brand and shrink your business to a very profitable margin—with no sales and no new customers.

For example, you might look at situations in which you have lower sales and market share but very high profits. In this case, it might be preferable to try to increase market share by lowering margin dollars and operating profits. A slight adjustment in profitability might result in a large increase in demand for your product, ultimately resulting in more margin dollars and more total profits. Big companies will run sophisticated elasticity studies on price and margins. Guided by intuition, most companies experiment their way into the optimal mix of sales and profitability.

TIP

Look beyond simple sales trends. Explore the underlying usage habits of your customers and those of your industry.

Sales trends tell you a lot about customer preferences. However, there is another level of analysis that will provide you with important insights when you start developing strategy—product and service usage habits. Your products are purchased for specific reasons, some may be the same as competitive offerings and some may be very different. Famous Footwear customers spend very little time in the store relative to the DSW shopper. The two retailers share many of the customers, yet they shop each retailer for vastly different reasons and occasions. DSW is about the thrill of the hunt and Famous Footwear is about the thrill of the find. The DSW customer shops the store for herself and often considers her experience there as recreational shopping. The Famous Footwear shopping occasion is primarily a family shopping trip, often with kids along. Here ease, success, and the ability to get in and out in a reasonable amount of time are paramount.

Now think about automobiles. All cars get people from Point A to B, but the use and occasion reasons vary by brand. The use differences between Jeep, Lexus, and Smart (from Daimler AG) vehicles are obvious. Understanding the usage or occasion differences of your customers will allow you to develop product, service, and communication strategies that relate directly to why your customers choose you over other competitors. As a result, you will be reinforcing your brand differences and help to create an even more meaningful brand experience.

Awareness and Attitudes

Track your company's and your individual product's awareness and the attitudes toward your brands relative to your key competitors. Both of these measures are critical scorecards for your company and, when viewed over time, provide insight into the health of your company and its brands.

We feel that this area is important enough to provide a more detailed discussion that can be found in Appendix A. We strongly encourage you to read and study the consumer behavior model found in Appendix A and to apply the insights gained from this approach as you market your business.

Gathering Information on Distribution

At a football game, a hot dog in the stands can cost twice what it costs if you leave your seat and go to the concession stand. The concession stand price may be five times the price of what you would pay if you prepared the hot dog yourself at home. If you are hungry and enjoying the game, you are willing to pay for the convenience of getting the hot dog in your seat.

How efficiently and effectively your product or service gets into the hands of your customer can make or break your business. It is important to understand the dynamics of your key distribution channels and their trends over time.

Distribution is about getting your product or service to your customer when they want it, how they want it, and at a price they are willing to pay. When you are getting started on your marketing plan, it is important to understand the dynamics of your distribution channels. Which channels are used most by your customers? Which channels are growing the fastest in the industry? Is your brand growing faster or slower in these channels? Why? How are your key competitors doing in these channels? Are there any emerging distribution channels, such as online selling, that you should consider penetrating?

TIP

Review your channel of distribution trends over a five-year period. Changes in distribution often occur over several years. A single-year snapshot doesn't show movement and the development of a shift in either a market or in a brand's use of distribution channels.

Understand your market share within each of the channels you use. If you are weak in a given distribution channel relative to your key competitors, it could be that they have a product offering more suited to that channel (e.g., club stores) or that they have stronger relationships with key retailers in these channels. If you don't have enough market coverage, your mass marketing efforts will be inefficient. Historically, large package goods companies launching new products have chosen to wait until they have at least a 60 percent weighted distribution on the product before beginning expensive proposition mass advertising.

TIP

How you sell your products or service is part of your distribution; your distribution strategy can be a key source of competitive advantage.

It is often useful to examine how you sell your product relative to your competition. You might use an independent rep system, an in-house sales force, a broker network, or depend exclusively on wholesalers. Each has its advantages, but you need to be able to link up the advantages it provides with what's important to your customers.

Professional auto mechanics only get paid when they are working on a car. It is critical for them to have the right tools to complete jobs quickly. If a tool breaks or gets lost, the time it takes to go to the store and replace it can result in lost income for the mechanic and the shop. Snap-On Tools recognized that mechanics didn't have time to shop for tools. They built a distribution model with franchisees driving trucks loaded with tool inventories directly to the mechanics. Their tools sell for a significant premium and have a reputation as being the best in the business. If they had tried to build their business through the traditional retail channels, they would not have been so successful.

Dell Computers also created a competitive advantage by figuring out how to build and ship computers directly to the consumer, bypassing the traditional distribution channels. Tupperware created a unique direct distribution model, bringing products directly to the homes of millions of consumers via fun parties thrown by friends.

Subway now has more restaurant locations than McDonald's, because it created a totally different distribution strategy. Instead of exclusive freestanding locations, Subway aggressively partnered with interstate filling stations, fitness centers, school cafeterias, and other nontraditional locations that all had one thing in common—lots of traffic.

The companies in these examples looked at distribution as a potential competitive advantage. They studied how best to get their product to their customers when, where, and how the customers wanted it. When you are building your distribution strategy, consider the disadvantages of the current distribution system and the needs of your customers. How have other industries satisfied similar needs and wants of their consumers? Can you translate this learning to your situation?

TIP

Your distribution should be consistent with your brand positioning —remember that the cheapest distribution channel may not be the best if you have a premium brand.

If your product or service is about convenience, don't locate in a mall. If it's about personal service, don't depend on a rep firm to sell your products, but consider building your own sales force: one that receives an incentive for what you want to be known for—great service.

Many brands must deliver a unique brand experience to their customers, requiring greater control of the distribution. For example, Starbucks does a great job of making customers feel rewarded when relaxing over Venti Mocha. Their employees receive ample training and enjoy good healthcare benefits. Their shops are not cheaply decorated. Starbucks does all this because it knows it needs to create a positive experience for its customers.

On the other hand, one could argue that selling Starbucks ice cream in the freezer bin of the grocery channel detracts from the overall image of the brand, because there is no experience attached to the purchase or consumption.

Gathering Pricing Information

How should you price your product or service? Companies use many approaches. In most established categories, there is a set of competitors with entrenched price points that dictate the range of prices into which you must fit. In the information-gathering stage, you will need to know what key competitors are charging, which price segments are growing, and which retail channels require distinct pricing strategies. At most big-box retailers, you will find a pricing strategy of "good, better, best."

Similar to product and distribution, you will gain tremendous consumer behavior insight by tracking sales and profit (gross margin dollars) by the different price lines across your major products and product categories. A price line is nothing more than the different price zones for which a product can be purchased in your industry. For example, shoes can be purchased for under $20, $21 to $50, $51 to $80, $81 to $110, and over $110.

TIP

Make sure the price points at which you sell are consistent with the positioning you develop for your product. A high price point suggests a premium product. If that is what you intend to communicate, make sure your sales are coming from higher price points than the industry as a whole.

Spend time analyzing whether the price you are charging for your products or your company's services matches that of your positioning. Remember, price is always a factor, but it is rarely the determining factor in a consumer's decision process. The business world is filled with examples of success tied to raising the price to communicate a better product. Do you think Corona or Michelob costs any more than Miller High Life to produce and distribute? In the beer business, it's common to find a regional beer charging higher prices the farther it gets away from its point of distribution. In its day, Old Style was an inexpensive beer in the Midwest, where most of its distribution occurred, but it was a premium beer in the South. Where it was priced high, its quality perception was much higher than in the areas of the country where it was a competitively-priced beer.

TRAP

Ignoring your competition's pricing can be detrimental. Set up a review of your competitors' pricing during the year. Simple shopping trips throughout the year can provide you with insight into what your competitors are doing and provide the basis for decisions on whether you want to follow what they are doing or diverge from it.

If there are price lines that are growing significantly more than your company's price lines are growing, review why this is happening, and determine whether you need to increase your presence there. If you are a mass player and depend upon volume, you will need to stay within the price lines that account for the most volume. However, if you intend to be more of a niche player and differentiate around quality or some other attribute that allows for a higher price, you will need to make sure your sales are in price lines consistent with this strategy.

Try to understand the price sensitivity of your company's customers and the consumers in your industry. Customers can tell you a lot about the strength of your products relative to competitive offerings. Consumer demand changes as prices are increased and decreased. Study the times your company has fluctuated its prices either up or down and determine this effect on volume and margin dollars.

Does a modest increase in price above that of your competition do little to stifle demand for your product but result in additional margin and margin dollars? If this is the situation, you have a strongly differentiated product that consumers are purchasing for reasons other than purely price.

Do you compete in a fairly undifferentiated marketplace, in which a decrease in price would bring about lower margins, but enough additional top-line sales volume to result in incremental margin dollars?

Two things affect price sensitivity most:

1. *Brand relevance.* If the customers purchasing your brand do so because of superior attributes or some other more intangible connection that you've established over time, they will be far less price sensitive. On the other hand, if you have an undifferentiated, parity brand, you will find more price sensitivity and elasticity. There is only one coffee shop in many people's minds and that's Starbucks. Within reason, they can raise prices without a fall-off in demand, especially since competitors will closely watch, and often follow, the leader's pricing strategy.

2. *Brand differentiation.* In many instances, the more intangible or differentiated your brand, the less price sensitivity exists. Service firms are

very good examples. Why does one law firm, one advertising agency, or one insurance firm charge premium prices? It's difficult to determine the value of many of these firms relative to other competitors except from intangible signals, such as the look of the office, the dress of the individuals, and the reputation of the firm.

Understanding Market Trends

Every market is constantly changing, and good marketers need to understand these changes. Every trend brings with it opportunity and threats to the marketer. The athletic shoe industry has experienced many industry trends that have affected the business.

- The steep growth of participation in popular sports in the 1960s and 1970s led to specialized shoes. Instead of a "gym" shoe, there evolved running shoes, basketball shoes, aerobic shoes, tennis shoes, and many other shoes for specific occasions.

- Recently, the advent of "sports fusion" shoes has changed the athletic shoe business again. In the 1980s though the early 2000s, athletic shoes represented fashion as much as they did sport. The introduction of the new Air Jordans were events with long lines of people waiting to get the most recent Nike product. Athletic shoes defined street fashion to suburban fashion. Athletic shoes were worn for sport, for "kicking around," and even for nights on the town. Enter the new Euro Sport of Sports Fusion shoes—athletic-inspired casual shoes. Today, runners use their running shoes for their early Saturday morning jog. But after the shower, the athletic shoes stay in the closet.

Both of these examples show how industry trends can affect consumer demand. Companies like Nike, Adidas, and New Balance all understood the first trend and built empires by following product segments and consumer segments that used the specific sports' shoes. In the second example, many of these same companies missed the trend and their business was negatively affected—while companies like Skechers, who jumped on the sports fusion trend early, became market leaders in the category and built huge businesses during this trend.

Understand the demographic trends affecting your business. Demographics include things like:

- Age of consumers

- Income of consumers

- Education levels of consumers

- Family composition of consumers, such as female-headed household, number of people per household, presence of children, and number of children

- Ethnicity of consumers

Most companies are affected by these demographics. If you are a realtor, the growth of key demographics in a given city will predict demand for housing in the future. If you sell a product related to retirement or primary education, the age of the population now and in the future will help predict your success and help you decide whether your product offering needs to evolve to meet the changes.

TIP

Become an expert on the future. Pick the one or two most important consumer trends to your business and stay up on them. Consumer trends provide another level of insight into consumer demand that can help you make smart decisions about whom to market to and what products your business should market.

IDEO, one of the leading product design and development firms in the country, uses an approach by which they project what a consumer's life will be like for five to ten years, and then they brainstorm ideas from this future perspective.

Trends such as activities, purchase trends, attitudes toward aging, time pressures, apparel, accessories, body piercing, health, food, environment, recreation, sex and dating, education, economics, social and business etiquette, and many others, may be relevant. Choose the one or two trends that you feel are most important to your business and make it a habit to stay up on them.

One key trend in the baby care category was a shift among moms away from the use of bar soaps to liquid soaps for bathing babies. The bar soaps were perceived as less gentle and convenient. Rather than fight this trend, Johnson & Johnson accelerated it with new product launches, including a "Head-to-Toe" baby wash for both bathing and shampooing. Today, bar soaps for babies are rarely used.

There are many easily accessible magazines and Web sites to help you track consumer trends relevant to your business.

- Faith Popcorn and her firm, BrainReserve. Faith has published several books on future trends. You can contact her at Faithpopcorn.com.

- Gerald Celente, of The Trends Research Institute and publisher of *The Trends Journal.* His Web site can be found at www.trendsresearch.com.

- Iconoculture (www.iconoculture.com). A research firm that tracks trends and acts as an extension of your team. They provide customers with a newsletter and customized searches across consumer insights and product categories.

- *The McKinsey Quarterly* (www.mckinseyquarterly.com). An extension of the McKinsey consulting firm.

- *American Demographics Magazine.* Dedicated to exploring demographic trends and their ramifications for American life and business.

- Nielsen's Buzzmetrics division hosts a free Web site called BlogPulse (www.blogpulse.com). It allows you to input any term and scours tens of thousands of blogs for comments using that search term.

It's important to follow the technological trends that will affect your customers and your business. We all know that technology is moving faster and faster. What used to be impossible yesterday is possible today: the ability to capture customer data for use in a customer relationship management program; use of sophisticated point-of-sale scanning equipment; productivity changes due to technological advances and manufacturing trends; or technology changes that will lead to new products and change the way you need to do business.

Understanding Your Competition

Good marketers have a solid understanding of their competitors and their strengths and weaknesses. It would be foolhardy for a small company to take a well-entrenched, well-resourced competitor head on. For years, many marketers have followed the tip below from Sun Tzu, the influential Chinese military strategist from the sixth century BC.

TIP

Target a weakness in your competitor's strength. A competitor's strength is something they will be incapable of changing. Study strengths to find weaknesses in your competitors.

This may seem counterintuitive, but if you think about it, it is a very powerful strategy. For example, McDonald's is perhaps the most efficient purveyor of mass-marketed fast food. They can serve a perfect hamburger and fries every time in a clean, friendly environment. Understanding this,

Burger King competes on a benefit that McDonald's model can't address: *having it your way,* or customizing your burger. Subway goes after a chink in the armor of both of these fast-food giants by celebrating the freshness and healthfulness of its sub sandwiches relative to the burger chains with its "eat fresh" tagline. Taco Bell asks us to "think outside the bun," because this is something the burger chains will never change.

Monitor both your primary and secondary competitors. All businesses have a primary and secondary set of competitors. It is helpful to define the key competitors with whom you compete—those that are most like you and serve the same customer profile, with the same shopping intent, with the same channel, with roughly the same price and product categories.

How Much Should We Spend on Advertising?

One trend that good marketers are especially keen to track is the advertising spending of their competitors. This is because in many markets the advertising *share of voice* will directionally equal the share of market over time. Directionally, we mean that you typically won't be number one in market share if you are number seven in share of voice. There are many exceptions to this rule of thumb, but generally speaking, the more awareness and

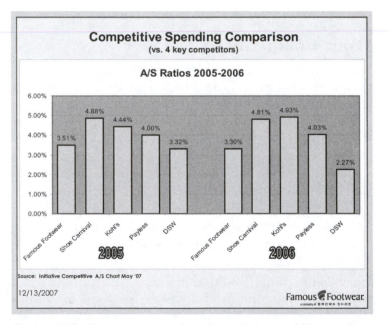

Figure 1.2. Competitive spending chart. Courtesy of Famous Footwear.

relevant differentiation a mass brand can build for itself through advertising, the greater its share of the market over time. There are various monitoring services that will track advertising spending for a fee.

Another key measure you may want to track is the *advertising-to-sales ratio*. In other words, how much are competitors spending to advertise their brands as a percentage of their sales? This is important to understand, because as you build a profit and loss statement, it can be a general guide to how much you will need to budget for advertising. The chart in Figure 1.2 is the way Famous Footwear, a major retailer of shoes, tracks its competitors' advertising-to-sales ratios.

In one sense, Coke competes directly with Pepsi in the "cola wars." Yet both companies are aware that when you are thirsty, you have many options besides cola. They consider themselves to be competing for "share of stomach" rather than cola market share. Because of this, they need to monitor what is going on in bottled waters, sports drinks, coffee, milk drinks, etc. In fact, both companies support brands in many of these segments.

Figure 1.3 is a template you can use to get a better sense of your competitors' strengths and weaknesses. The template is filled out with the example of a shoe retailer, Shoe Carnival.

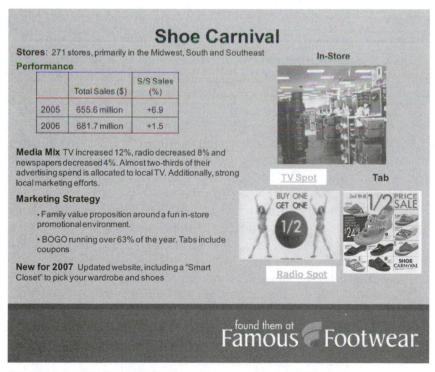

Figure 1.3. Competitive template. Courtesy of Famous Footwear.

Understanding Your Company History and Culture

The information you need to develop a strong marketing program is not just external. Every company has a history. Understanding the history of your company and its products gives you tremendous insights into the brand—insights you'll use in marketing your business. What stories do employees tell about how the company was founded? What were some of the biggest challenges the company had to overcome and how did it overcome them? What was the founder like? What sort of charities does your company support? What kinds of people do well at your company? What does this tell you about the culture?

It's important to remember that where you've been is usually where you are going. The internal, "tribal" stories are critical to understand, because today, marketing needs to be honest and authentic. The first people to see through a company telling an inauthentic marketing story are its employees. If they can't get behind it, how are they going to convince a customer to connect with their offering?

Naturalizer: A Brand That Temporarily Lost its Way

In the 1950s and early 1960s, the Naturalizer brand was the only brand that was targeted directly to women via national advertising. Its basic promise was both comfort and great fashion, and the brand essence was brought to life through the famous Leo Burnett advertising campaign with the tagline, "a beautiful fit." However, in the 1980s and 1990s, the brand strayed from its roots. Naturalizer was nearly forgotten and then nearly killed after a brand manager tried to revive the brand. The brand went younger, it went sexier, it tried to become cutting edge fashion, and it changed whenever the next photographer had another idea about what the shoe should be and how it should be portrayed (see Figure 1.4).

With a management change, the marketers went back to basics. They went back through the history of the brand and worked hard to understand what it stood for and why it was loved in the first place. In addition, through consumer research, they discovered that those reasons still resonated with the brand today. The Naturalizer brand was and still is about comfortable fashion. It does best with a target market of "the woman who is comfortable with herself." She wants fashion but won't be a slave to it. She demands comfort along with style. It was this understanding of the brand's original positioning and essence that led to the brand's re-emergence as one of the leading women's shoe brands today. The brand is once again the leading department store brand, and is profitable as well (see Figure 1.5).

Figure 1.4. Naturalizer: A brand that lost its way. Courtesy of Naturalizer, Mathias Vriens, photographer.

Figure 1.5. Naturalizer: Back on brand. Courtesy of Naturalizer, Pamela Hansen, photographer.

The Nike shoe was created by Bill Bowerman, a track coach at Oregon University, to help his star, Steve Prefontaine, perform better. The brand is still is about performance today.

Chevrolet was created to be an affordable quality car for Americans. Some of the first ads had Doris Day singing about seeing the USA in a Chevrolet. The company has been very consistent in telling this story, even through the current campaign with its "An American Revolution," tagline.

The Ogilvy advertising agency was founded by David Ogilvy, who was originally a market researcher. The agency pioneered advertising based on consumer insights and research. This remains an important driver of the agency today. All brands have a story that's rooted in their history if you dig deep enough. Spend time to understand your company's past. It helps create the future.

Capture your company's story. Ask:

- What's your company's history?
- Who were the important leaders, what were they like, and what mattered to them?
- What were the defining challenges they faced?
- What's your company's culture like? What does the company value?
- What were the major successes and why?
- What failures happened along the way and why?
- How has your industry changed over the years? How did your company react to these changes?

Understanding the Language of Your Category

Every company has its own set of arcane acronyms and phrases. At my first job, they kept talking about BFD. To me it meant something totally inappropriate, until I found out they meant "Best Food Day" (the best day to run a food ad in the local paper). It is easy to get sucked into the trap of using "marketing speak" as you develop your marketing strategies for your customer communication. Remember that your customer doesn't think this way.

TRAP

Don't be an outsider. Ignore the "code" and you won't be able to communicate effectively. Understand and use the language of your target and you will connect with them as one of them.

Every category has its own "code" language of unique words and phrase that connect the users to each other. Understanding the meaning and importance of words is one of the keys to understanding your customer and marketing your business. Every business, every occupation, every recreation, every culture, even every set of friends have specific sets of words that are particular to the group.

Have you ever participated in a triathlon? If you have, you know what the words listed below mean. Even if you recognize some of them, you probably can't truly comprehend the meaning and spirit of the words unless you're an "insider" and actually participate or are part of the tribe that lives triathlons.

- T-1
- T-2
- Zip wheels
- 76-degree seat post
- Bonking
- Gu
- Anaerobic versus aerobic training
- Body marking
- Transition area
- Intervals
- Zone 1,2,3,4,5
- Aero position

Now think of Starbucks. The Italian words Grande, Venti, and Frappuccino are all unique to the retailer of coffee. They are purposely used to suggest a sense of quality and taste. Understanding their meaning and how customers relate to them is one of the keys to understanding the target market. Nothing is less cool than an adult brand trying to appeal to a younger target, while not understanding the "code" language. Words are the language of understanding. They unlock very important meaning to your customers. Know the "code."

TIP

Identify your company and customer rituals. Understand what they mean and why they are important.

In our family, we have a little ritual to make birthdays special for the kids. We bring out the brightly-colored "birthday plate" and the birthday girl gets her favorite meal cooked for her. One day, the "birthday plate" fell and broke. The kids insisted on gluing it back together, rather than getting a new one. It's a simple little thing, but our kids would be crushed if we stopped this tradition.

When you think back on your childhood, what do you especially remember? Working on a project with your dad? A family gathering? A traumatic event? Chances are, those key memories are also associated with strong emotions. We only truly learn things when there is emotion. We only really remember things when there is emotion. When brands understand this and are able to connect with these emotions, they become truly iconic.

Every company has rituals that make it special to their customers. Whether it is the presentation of merchandise when you open the smiling package delivered from Amazon, or the ritual of ordering at Starbucks, then moving to the end of the counter where the unique name of your drink is called and you lovingly place a sleeve over the cup before you take a sip. Rituals define cultures and we all take part in them. Most people are involved in weddings, funerals, birthday parties, engagements, and bachelor parties. The morning shower, the walk to the mailbox to pick up the Sunday paper, going to the ballgame with your kids—these are all rituals that define our lives. Good marketers are keen observers of these rituals and how their brands fit into these rituals.

Your customers have repeated experiences with your business. Maybe it's the way you engage them when they call for customer service, or how they are greeted when they walk into your store, or the yearly "thank you party" you throw for your vendors or suppliers, or how you conduct a sales call—all these are rituals that help define who you are and how you do business.

Spend a little time to make sure you capture the rituals of your company and those of your competitors. Celebrate your rituals and make them part of your customers' interactions with your company.

As mentioned above, the purpose of this section is simply to gather information that you will use in marketing your business. You don't have to be judgmental or think about how to make your rituals more powerful at this point, just understand them. We'll show you how to use this information in subsequent chapter.

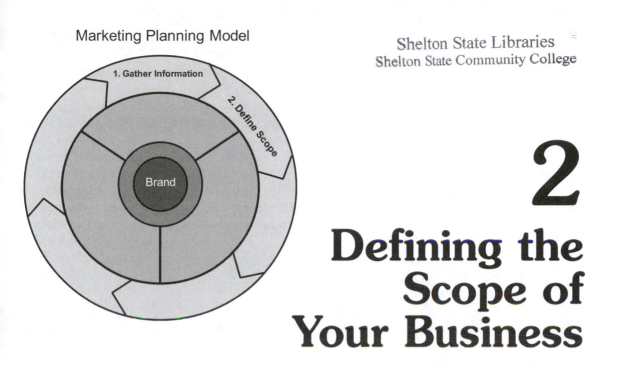

2

Defining the Scope of Your Business

You only have to do a very few things right in your life, so long as you don't do too many things wrong.
—Warren Buffett

What Business Are You In?

You've probably been asked the question many times: "What business are you in?" This question is often difficult to answer. Many business leaders can never truly articulate what it is they produce that consumers love. Sometimes, they simply practice under old assumptions.

Consumer tastes change, technology changes, and competition changes. These changes often result in a foundation that moves out from underneath a business. Over time, the business you're in may change but if your company is still working under the old assumptions, you won't be able to effectively market your business. Some businesses never fully realize the true business they are in and undermine the chances of effectively marketing their business. Think about the following three examples:

1. Xerox was in the copy machine business during the 1960s. Over time it became a *document company*, as copy machines gave way to faxes and faxes gave way to transferring data over the Internet. Moving from being a copy machine company to a document company meant the business had to be marketed differently.

27

2. If you have a daughter, niece, or granddaughter, chances are you've heard of American Girl, the high-end doll brand. Most people would assume that the company that makes these dolls, the Pleasant Company, would be in the toy business. But founder Pleasant Rowland never defined her business as a doll business. She always saw the company as being in the *education business*. Dolls are the vehicle, but the business is about educating young girls. Toward that end, American Girl has a complete set of well-researched historical dolls that come to life through publications and accessories. The new dolls in the collection are often introduced during events that take place at the historical locations where the dolls' characters originated, providing the perfect setting to help girls bond with the history and backgrounds of their new dolls.

3. Much has been written about Starbucks. The easy answer to what business they are in would be the coffee business. However, Howard Schultz, founder and CEO of Starbucks, has stated that he is not in the coffee business, serving people, but rather in the *people* business, serving *coffee*. Starbuck's is in the business of *offering people a little reward in the third location* (the other two being home and business). Starbucks is about an experience. It's a pause in the day that is all yours. It's about stealing a little time for yourself in an environment that connects with you. It's about the music they play, the way you order your coffee, the chairs you sit in, the plug-in for your computer, and the people you see there. It's about the experience—a rewarding experience.

This chapter will help you define what business you are in, your focus for competing, and the direction for the product or service areas you will develop and market.

So, what business *are* you in? What's the scope of your business? It's not about how you're better, but how your business profitably provides people with a product or service they want, when and how they want it.

Determining Strengths and Weaknesses

Strengths are internal advantages you have that help you compete for business through increasing your market share and profitability relative to the competition. Weaknesses are the opposite—they cause your organization to be at a disadvantage with respect to your competition and they are potentially the reason for a future loss in market share and profitability.

TIP

Look for clusters of strengths from multiple areas of your business that suggest an area of dominance.

At what can you be the best in the world? This may sound like a high bar to set for your company, but in today's world it is a necessity. As Thomas Friedman has pointed out—the world is "flat"—meaning that every business ultimately competes in a global marketplace. Every company needs to specialize in something they can win at on a global scale. Clusters of strengths will ultimately provide you with the insight to your core competency and what business you're in. Clusters of strengths could be three to five strengths that all really point to the same thing. Nike has superior technology, access to the best athletes in the world, and a heritage that comes from one of its founders, coach Bowerman. These three strengths have the common defining element of *performance.*

Force yourself to think about the entire spectrum of possibilities. List as many strengths and weaknesses as you can across the major components of your business. Then ask yourself, *can we be the best in the world at any of these?* Whether you like it or not, you are competing against companies from around the world. The following are some places to look for strengths and weaknesses:

Product

Consider product strengths and weaknesses that your company could own versus the competition. For example:

- *Superior materials* (Volvo cars, known for superior construction)
- *Company heritage* and reputation in the industry and category (Federal Express)
- *Implied endorsement* from experts (Lance Armstrong for Trek bikes)
- *Warranties* (Sam's Club, Marshall Fields, Nordstrom, and LL Bean—all known for their generous return and exchange policies)
- *Unique product attributes* (Dawn dishwasher soap—it not only cleans dishes but gets out stains)

Distribution

Are there distribution strengths and advantages your company has over the competition that are meaningful to your customers and the consumers in your industry category? For example:

- Geographic exclusivity. Can you dominate a certain territory?
- More experienced and knowledgeable rep force.
- In-house sales force when everyone else is using agents or reps.
- Use of an emerging channel that is gaining acceptance with the consumers in your industry (example the Internet, catalogs, mid/value tier in retail).
- Superior shelf-space and the ability to control shelf-space (if you are in the consumer goods business).
- Favorable locations and flexible leases (if you are in the retail business).

Pricing

Are there unique pricing advantages or disadvantages that pertain to your company? If you decide you want to be the low-price leader in a category, you will need to have the lowest cost structure to succeed in the long run. Here are some places to look for pricing/cost advantages:

- Lower operating efficiencies.
- Patent protection.
- High price elasticity of your company's product. The lower gross margin (sales less cost of goods sold) from lower prices results in more demand and a net result of higher total margin dollars due to the increase in overall demand.

Marketing

Are there unique marketing advantages or disadvantages that pertain to your company? For example:

- Strong brand equity position.
- Domination of consumer awareness.
- Strong brand connection to specific consumer or business-to-business target markets, as measured by share of market, repeat purchase rates, consumer research, and willingness to recommend product or service measures.
- Favorable customer service strategy.
- Superior customer database and customer relationship management program.
- Unique product differentiation in the consumers' minds as measured through consumer research.

Technology

Consider the technology advances and then decide if these are an opportunity or a risk to your firm. State these in terms of advantages and disadvantages that pertain to your company. Some example situations follow:

- Superior inventory management practices.
- New material, such as when Gore-Tex came on the market.
- New attribute or better way of doing things, such as the Swiffer Mop.
- Addition to make an existing product better, such as a medicine-coated stent.

Target Market and Trends

Consider the target market and consumer trends, and then decide if these are an opportunity or a risk to your firm. State these in terms of advantages and disadvantages that pertain to your company. For example:

- Consumers' lack of time and need for convenience.
- Younger age groups getting more of their news from the Internet and less from the traditional newspaper.
- The emergence of Facebook and YouTube as major communication portals.
- Increasingly active lifestyle of older Americans, as evidenced by magazines like *Masters Athlete*, a magazine for "geezerjocks."
- Emergence and success of mid-tier department stores away from the malls, such as Kohl's and JC Penny.

W. Chan Kim and Renée Mauborgne, authors of *Blue Ocean Strategy*, provide a powerful framework for thinking about how to identify *new* category drivers, with good examples of companies that were successful in leveraging these to their advantage.

Determine Your Core Competency

Now that you've thought about your firm's strengths and weaknesses, you can turn to analyzing your firm's core competency. The core competency is the basis for determining what business you are in and in what industry you will compete. Core competencies are enabled by the underlying strengths of the organization. A core competency must:

- Define and provide a perceived customer benefit.
- Be the reason or common set of abilities the company can provide the customer benefit better than the competition.
- Be truly differentiating and difficult to copy.

Core competencies take a lot of work to figure out. Think of core competencies as the roots of a tree. The roots provide the foundation for the tree and the system of sustaining the tree through nutrient delivery. That's what core competencies do for businesses. Core competencies provide boundaries—within which hiring of talent is judged, development of products is measured, funding of marketing programs is determined, and operational business strategies are developed. However, while the branches are visible, the roots are not. In a business, the visible components are things like the products, the offices, the people, and the advertising campaigns and taglines. But the core competencies stay in the background, providing the support for all the visible aspects of a business. Think about the following businesses:

- *Anheuser-Busch:* The maker of Budweiser, the king of beers. What's Anheuser-Busch's core competency? Is it the taste of its beer, the power of the advertising, the ability to introduce new products, or it's sheer size? Ask anyone in the beer industry who competes against the giant and they'd tell you very quickly—it's their *distribution system.* The beer producer has a system of experienced distributors, who solely distribute the Budweiser product to retailers and taverns. The outcome—Budweiser gets total attention and support and doesn't have to "fight" to get the attention of their distributors. As a result, Budweiser can introduce new products, get shelf space with retailers, and execute marketing programs far more efficiently and effectively. Its competition isn't so lucky. They often split distributors, with the result that powerful distributors sell multiple brands. The King of Beers is the king, not because of its product, but because of the unique and powerful distribution system it has created.

- *Black & Decker:* Black & Decker makes literally hundreds of products with its name on them. However, the firm defines its core competency as *the ability to make a better motor.* As a result, while the most visible aspect of Black & Decker is the many power tools with the brand name, the firm is actually much more prevalent than you might think. Yes, they are dominant in power tools, such as sanders and drills. But they also make the major component of household cleaning tools, such as the Dustbuster and kitchen appliances, and the motors in food processors. The company's core competency is *motors* with the end product simply being the housing for a great motor.

- *Procter & Gamble:* At business school, students study many cases involving the marketing giant Procter & Gamble. However, marketing is not their core competency—that's much too broad a way to describe a core competency. It's two aspects of marketing that make up Procter & Gamble's core competency. Over the years, the packaged goods giant has been the best in the world at identifying *consumer insights* through marketing research and talking and listening to consumers. This, coupled with a historically superior *brand portfolio management* capability, has fueled the company's growth and profitability. The company pioneered brand management and then, during the early 1990s, recognized that individual products could be grouped under target market managers. This resulted in efficiencies and great effectiveness of both insights and marketing expenditures. The company's ability to manage a portfolio of products has kept it at the forefront through developing products based on customer insights that have unique reasons for being and that support and complement the existing Procter & Gamble product lines.

We started this chapter by stating that Xerox is in the document business, American Girl is in the education business, and Starbucks is in the business of giving customers a little reward in a pleasant third location. Anheuser Busch is really in the distribution business, Black & Decker is in the motor business, and Procter & Gamble is in the consumer insight and product portfolio management business. Determining your business's core competency is the direct link to answering the question—what business are you in?

TRAP

Most businesses do not have more than one core competency. This is an easy trap to fall into. You get too close to your business and think that you are great at everything. Be very discerning here. You're lucky if you have one core competency, because very few businesses really are great at multiple things. In today's "flat" world, the key question is, at what can you be best in the world?

It's the combinations of strengths and not any one individual strength that provide the insights into your core competency, which in turn provides the insight into what business you are in.

Perhaps the best way to demonstrate this is to use an example we worked on. The client was AAA, the massive automobile club. AAA provides roadside assistance to over 20 million customers in the United States alone. But it also provides a range of financial services ranging from loans to credit cards. The membership organization is a powerful provider of insurance, with a host of products that range from car insurance to life insurance. Different clubs specialized in different aspects of the product offerings. California had a strong travel orientation. The New York club was known for roadside assistance. Michigan had a strong insurance orientation. None of them combined the products to form a single guiding direction.

When AAA analyzed their strengths and weaknesses, a number of clusters started to emerge as their core competencies:

- Target market behavior was changing to shorter trips—a strength of AAA.
- In a complex business, AAA had superior management of the tow truck network in comparison to competitive offerings.
- There was a shift in roadside assistance toward inclusion of the service with the purchase of new cars. So another competitor was on the horizon who provided customers with this service through the purchase of a car, rather than in a secondary transaction after the purchase of a car. Therefore, AAA would not be able to dominate roadside assistance as it had in the past.
- AAA had a strong land package, air package, cruise package, and road travel capability. Furthermore, the organization had unique travel products with ties to other travel destinations, such as the Disney theme parks. Finally, it was known for directional support via their Triptiks, and for a full spectrum of travel information.
- AAA could bundle products to make superior travel packages (e.g., travel insurance, trip insurance, trip packages, and Triptik information) to create added value.
- AAA had an established branch system—brick and mortar and Internet presence—making them a multichannel travel retailer. In addition, there was a consistency in the way products and services were delivered.
- AAA had strong brand recognition and trust among consumers.

The final list was exhaustive, with pages of strengths and weaknesses that were captured from both top management, mid-level management, and customers. When analyzing the strengths and weaknesses, it started to become clear that AAA was in the business of being a *member travel organization*. AAA was not an individual seller of roadside assistance, or insurance, or travel products—but an organization that could bundle together travel for its members. To compete against the emerging competition in the different business categories in which AAA competed, the key was to view the organization as a unified entity against unbundled competitors. A member travel organization would build on the AAA strengths, provide value-added products versus a price orientation, and take advantage of the uniqueness of the AAA organization.

TIP

After you've decided upon your core competency, make sure you have what it takes to be successful in the core competency and in the business in which you've determined that you can best compete.

Make sure the core competency truly delivers a customer benefit and is difficult for competitors to imitate.

Once we looked at the potential core competency that would answer the question as to the business of AAA, we went through a check to see if we were correct in our assumptions. We listed all the things that a business focusing on being a member travel organization would need to succeed. We then went back to the list of strengths and weaknesses and checked to see what was needed. Table 2.1 is a brief example of that work:

Table 2.1. Member Travel Organization

Necessary for success	Strength	Weakness
Large loyal membership	X	
Recognized strength in travel	X	
Broad array of travel products across travel options, information, insurance, and financial	X	
Ability to bundle products	X	
History of marketing bundled products not selling individual products		X
Linkages of offices and information	X	
Unique relationships with travel destinations	X	
Knowledgeable travel counselors	X	
Operational focus of one company		X

As a last step, we reviewed Table 2.1 and the core competencies. For each line, we asked ourselves, "How difficult would it be for competitors to imitate what's needed to succeed in what are, ultimately, *our* core areas of competency?"

In conclusion, when determining what AAA's core competency was, the organization didn't pick any one product. Instead, AAA picked the consumer benefit they specialized in that served as the link to all their travel products. AAA's core competency was that it was a *member travel organization.* Their core competency was serving members on the go. They provided their members with an overall travel experience few could rival, from credit cards, to car insurance, to creating actual travel experiences for its members.

Finally, in considering the scope of your business, ask yourself the question: *Beyond the things we are selling, what are we really marketing?* Every company sells something. Campbell's sell soup. Johnson & Johnson sells baby shampoo. But seen from a deeper perspective, Campbell's is really marketing a feeling of comfort and Johnson's a feeling of caring and nurturing. Companies that can define their scope on an emotional benefit level often have a more intimate connection with their customers and a broader scope of markets they can enter.

Marketing Planning Model

1. Gather Information

2. Define Scope

Brand

3. Define Brand

3
Defining
Your Brand

Products are made in the factory, but brands are created in the mind.
—Walter Landor

What Is Your Relevant Differentiation?

You are hungry. You are driving down the highway and you see the golden arches of McDonald's. Quick, what happens? Depending on who you are, you may pull off at the exit thinking about a cheeseburger and fries. Or you may think to yourself, now would be a good time for the kids to visit the restroom. Or you may think to yourself, I'd rather stay hungry until I find a place where I can get some healthier food. All of these are reactions to the symbols of the brand that McDonald's has created. In branding, we are trying to evoke the reaction that favors our brand.

Whatever your reaction is to the golden arches, you may notice that it is partly rational and partly emotional—we feel something about McDonald's. A brand that does not evoke some kind of feeling doesn't exist very long. The effect may be subtle, but we have an emotional relationship with every brand we regularly purchase in a supermarket. We have a feeling about it.

Note something else about your reaction—you don't think too deeply about the meaning of "McDonald's." You simply react. As much as we would like to believe that consumers are deeply attached to our brands, they happen to be very busy people with a lot on their minds. Thousands of other brands are competing for their attention every day. Imagine yourself at a big party, with lots of people you know and some you don't. You flit through the party and chat briefly with the familiar faces. You gravitate toward the people you enjoy and with whom you share similar outlooks. Our relationship to brands is very much like this party. We connect with them briefly for a time and then we are on to something else. In this busy and confusing environment, it is critical that your brands establish some kind of emotional connection with your customer to be successful.

The Financial Value of a Brand

In this country, we don't ascribe any tangible value to brands in the balance sheet. Any tangible brand value is incorporated into *goodwill*. In the UK, brands are treated as tangible assets. Most CEOs today view their brands as valuable assets and they manage them this way. There are some businesses for which the brand is the most valuable part of the business. Interbrand, a branding company in New York, publishes a list each year of the most valuable brands in the country and in the world. They have a sophisticated model by which they derive these valuations. If you buy into their methodology, Table 3.1 shows you the dollar value they have estimated for some key brands. If you compare this brand value to the market capitalization of the companies, the brands of some companies are worth nearly half the company value.

Table 3.1. The Value of a Brand

Brand	Value	% of Market Capitalization
Coca-Cola	$65 billion	45%
Microsoft	$59 billion	21%
IBM	$57 billion	36%
GE	$52 billion	12%

Source: Interbrand, 2007.

The value of the Coke brand is worth $67 billion. This is nearly half the value of the Coca-Cola company's market capitalization. Roberto Goizueta, the former CEO of the CocaCola Company, stated that if all of Coke's physical assets went away, they could still go to the bank and borrow over $60 billion because they own the Coke trademark. Why is it worth this much? What do they really own in the Coke brand? Coke shareholders can be pretty sure that tomorrow, all over the world, fans of Coke will go to the store and purchase it. They know what it tastes like and they like how it makes them feel.

How valuable is your brand? What percentage of the company's value does it comprise? Johnson & Johnson can charge $4 for a bottle of baby powder, while the comparable bottle from Walgreen's or CVS will cost $2.

Johnson's can charge twice as much because they have a powerful story to tell about the brand. You are not just buying talcum powder. When you buy a Johnson's product for your baby, you are buying gentleness and the feeling of being a good parent.

You can gain a ballpark estimate of your brand by comparing the value of your brand to a generic brand. Let's say you are selling a brand of hot dogs called "Beefy Dogs." How much more could you sell these for than a brand simply called "Joe's Hot Dogs"? How much more could you charge if the name of your hot dog were "Oscar Mayer"? It almost makes you wish you were an Oscar Mayer wiener!

What Makes a Strong Brand?

Write down a list of your favorite brands. What do they all have in common? Strong brands share many key traits, but there are six traits that distinguish most of them.

Strong Brands Are Well-Known

If I have never heard of your brand, it is hard for me to have any feelings about it. I don't know who you are, what you stand for, or what benefits you offer me. Simply building awareness of your brand can be a powerful way to grow it. Ten years ago, almost nobody had heard of a supplemental insurance brand called AFLAC. Today, you not only are aware of it, you probably get a smile on your face when the AFLAC duck comes to mind. The role that the duck campaign played in AFLAC's business growth is well documented. If you ever happen to be in the market for supplemental insurance, and you are offered three insurance brands, Jim's, Dave's, and AFLAC, you will naturally choose AFLAC. You have heard of them. They sound familiar. Therefore, they *must* be reputable.

Strong Brands Stay Relevant

Apple is a great example of a brand that has managed to stay relevant to its fans through a constant stream of amazing product innovations and very cool, very insightful advertising. All successful brands were relevant at one time, even Oldsmobile. The trick is staying relevant. Innovation in your products, services, and messaging go hand in hand. It is hard to make your brand relevant without some tangible news. Motorola was quickly losing the cell-phone battle to Nokia for a time. When they launched the RAZR phone and combined it with their "Hello Moto" campaign, it made the brand relevant again.

Strong Brands Are Differentiated from Their Competitors

Harley-Davidson motorcycles are not any faster, more reliable, or more efficient than other brands of motorcycles, but they sure are different. When you hear that "hog" sound, even before it comes around the corner you know that a Harley is coming.

Strong Brands Are Authentic

Authenticity has become more and more important as consumers have access to more information and have become more cynical about marketing messages. There was a time when you could just make up a brand story, like Betty Crocker, and consumers would relate to it. Today, we are much more cynical about such made-up stories. We connect much more readily with a retailer like REI, which was founded by folks who actually climbed mountains. Ben and Jerry started a wonderful little ice cream company in Vermont. A very authentic story. It will be interesting to see how the brand holds up now that the company is in the hands of Unilever.

Strong Brands Espouse a Worldview

When we do seminars on branding, we will often ask the audience if they believe that hunting promotes good family values. Most people line up pretty firmly on one side or the other. For hunters, it is a bonding experience and even a rite of passage for fathers and sons (and even for some mothers and daughters). For nonhunters, it can seem abhorrent. If you believe hunting promotes good family values, you are probably a big fan of Gander Mountain, a successful retailer for outdoorspeople. If you don't believe hunting is a good thing, you wouldn't be caught dead there.

The retailer Target subtly espouses the belief that you don't have to be rich to enjoy good design. This belief is shared by their customers. When Nike says, "just do it," they are sharing a belief that complaining and excuse-making don't help you get in shape or achieve athletic goals. Only hard work and sacrifice can get you there. For those lacing up Nike shoes to go for a run on a cold morning, it is a belief they truly understand.

Strong Brands Tell Stories That Connect Emotionally

Humans are storytellers. Since the beginning of time, we have been telling each other stories to explain the world. When there is information missing in the story, we fill it in. We create our own stories to explain the world.

We do the same thing with brands. A company gives us some clues about the brand—a product, an ad, an experience at the store—and we fill in the blanks to complete our story about the brand. The important thing is that this story exists in the mind of the customer, not in the marketing document of the company. Go back to that list of your favorite brands. Why are you loyal to them? What did they do to hook you? You may not even be able to express why you feel the way you do about them, but deep down they make you feel good about something. Maybe they remind you of a special time you had with your mom or dad, maybe they evoke an exciting time in your life.

Whatever the connection, strong brands understand this and strive to reinforce the emotional connections. Stories are one of the most powerful ways we have found to connect emotionally. The Green Bay Packers are one of the National Football League's best-loved franchises. Here is a team in the smallest market in the league, owned by the residents of Wisconsin. And yet they have had remarkable success. They are also a brand. The Packers consistently sell more merchandise nationally than most other teams in the NFL. For us, the Packers are more than a football team. They evoke memories of watching games on a little black-and-white TV with our dads during the Lombardi era. Consumers don't remember bullet points. They only remember facts when they are attached to a framework they understand. Stories are often your best framework.

TIP

Brand stories exist in the mind of the customer, not in your marketing plan. As much as we would like to believe that customers are internalizing all of our marketing messages, we can only hope that they retain a single key feeling or idea.

In every company for which we have worked, there has been a misperception that the customer understands the brand the way the marketing managers do. Unfortunately, they don't. The managers are much too close to the brand. Consumers don't have the time or the interest to care as much as you do. All that matters for your brand's success is the story your consumer takes away from your efforts.

Telling Your Brand's Story

Today, branding is interactive. Consumers create their own associations and stories about your brand. The best you can hope to do is guide this process by giving them clues and by helping them feel something for your brand. Consumers don't want to feel like they are being told a brand story. They

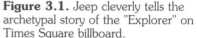

Figure 3.1. Jeep cleverly tells the archetypal story of the "Explorer" on Times Square billboard.

want to tell *themselves* the story. They want to be a part of the story. They don't want to consciously think about the brand story. They just want to enjoy it.

Jeep is a great example of a brand telling a consistent brand story. It is a story about discovery, about not being fenced in, about the desire to be free. How many cubicle-bound office workers long for this feeling of freedom? Jeep never tells you "we are the explorer." What they do is to give you clues about the brand's core story. Their campaign about "a new species of Jeep," which compares their new Wrangler Unlimited to a new species of tough beetles, gives us these clues about the explorer story. In Times Square, 20 stories up, they put a full-size replica of the new Jeep on a billboard that showed a flyswatter trying to stop it—unsuccessfully, of course (see Figure 3.1).

Archetypal Brand Stories

As we all know, there are good stories and bad stories. We usually quickly forget the bad ones. How do you tell a good brand story? One approach for telling a good story is to use the power of something called "archetypes."

Many companies have started using "archetypes" to build and guide their brand strategy. "Archetype" is a fancy word for a universal idea or concept shared by all humans. Archetypes are embodied in the classic stories that have been handed down to us from the beginning of human consciousness. C.J. Jung, a contemporary of Freud, is given credit for describing the power of archetypal stories. Joseph Campbell contributed greatly to the understanding of these powerful stories. Both men recognized the underlying patterns in archetypal stories. For example, the story of Achilles in Greek mythology, Siegfried in Germanic mythology, and Sampson from the Old Testament are basically the same story about the courage to overcome obstacles and achieving important things for themselves and others. These stories embody the archetypal story of the *hero*.

In their book, *The Hero and the Outlaw*, Carol Pearson and Margaret Mark describe 12 archetypal stories that brands have successfully used to guide their brand strategies. They very convincingly demonstrate that brands telling a single archetypal story have better long-term financial performance. Most of the companies we work with are guilty of telling either no story or multiple stories. This is confusing to your customers and your employees. A strong brand tells one story in a compelling way, over and over again. The 12 archetypes described by Pearson and Mark and the emotions on which they deliver, are listed in Table 3.2.

Table 3.2. Archetypes and Emotions

Hero	→	achievement
Lover	→	love
Rebel	→	rebellion
Sage	→	wisdom
Jester	→	enjoying the moment
Caregiver	→	nurturing
Ruler	→	power
Innocent	→	virtue
Creator	→	creativity
Explorer	→	freedom
Regular Guy/Gal	→	acceptance
Magician	→	transformation

We recognize these characters, stories, and archetypes immediately. Think of how many of these archetypal figures show up in the movies *Star Wars* or *Lord of the Rings*.

Every time Nike runs an ad, they are retelling the archetypal story of the *hero*. The *hero* story is about having the courage and drive to overcome significant

Figure 3.2. Plaque outside Niketown in Chicago

obstacles, to achieve, and ultimately to make the world a better place. Now, Nike never comes right out to claim to be the *hero* brand (a true hero would never do this!). But they do give you ample clues that let you come to this story on your own. Outside the Niketown store on Michigan Avenue in Chicago, there is a little plaque that eloquently captures this feeling of the *hero* (see Figure 3.2). One more cue for consumers to help build the brand story of Nike for themselves.

Brand Model

The following is a framework we have used to help companies understand and tell their brand story. We liken your brand to an iceberg (Figure 3.3).

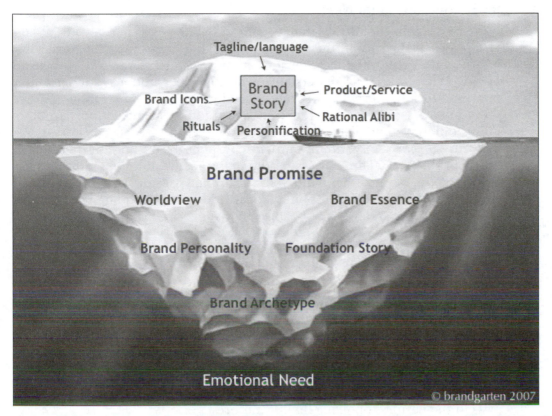

Figure 3.3. A brand model for understanding the key brand elements. Below the waterline are the elements internal to the company. Above the waterline are the elements your target sees.

Above the waterline are the things that consumers may come in contact with at some of the brand's key touch-points. Below the waterline are the strategic pillars internal to a company's brand, that help guide the strategy. The whole iceberg is geared to deliver on a single core emotion.

Below the Waterline:
Internal Branding Elements

There are some things your customers see about your brand, such as the logo and tagline. They can experience the product or service. But unless these things are guided by what is true about the culture of the company or brand, they will come across as inauthentic and inconsistent. The elements below are the things a company will identify to be true about its internal culture, before it tries to develop its external marketing strategy. They start from the bottom of the iceberg and work their way to the top. The following are the key steps.

Step 1: Identify the Emotional Need

The first step is identifying the key emotional need in your key target customer when they are in the process of thinking about your category. How do I want to feel when I am buying a tennis racquet, a car, a house, or an iPod? When you truly understand which single emotion your customer wants to feel, build your entire brand around delivering this emotion. Note that in any given category there may be up to four or five important emotions different brands could own. For example, in the cola category, Coke tells the *innocent* story with its authenticity, polar bears, and desire to teach the world to sing. This delivers on the emotional wish to be happy and virtuous. Pepsi, on the other hand, tells the archetypal story of the *jester*, which appeals to our wish to feel spontaneous and live in the moment. (For a list of key emotions, refer back to Table 3.2.)

TIP

Ask yourself what feeling your company is really selling—beyond the product or service it markets.

If you have a company that sells expensive watches, what are you really selling beyond the functional benefit of telling time? There is a story about the president of Rolex. Someone asked him how things were in the watch business. He replied that he had no idea, because he wasn't in the watch business—he was in the business of selling luxury and prestige.

You can't ask your customers directly how your brand makes them feel, so finding the emotional benefit is much harder than it might seem. In the consumer's logic, one purchases a watch to tell time. Realistically, how many Rolex-wearers would come right out and tell you that it makes them feel powerful? How many Mercedes drivers would admit to driving the car because it suggested to others they had "made it"? The keen observer will understand the true emotional reasons for a brand's attraction.

Step 2: Select the Archetypal Story That Delivers on This Emotion

This is the core story your brand will tell, and will be dictated by the emotion your brand is trying to own. Deep down, is your brand the *rebel*, the *hero*, the *lover*, or something else?

TIP

Identify the key emotional drivers first, then see which archetypal story your brand could own vs. your competition.

In many established categories, a few successful brands have already figured out that they own a key emotion and its corresponding archetypal stories. If this is the case, look for another relevant emotion you can win on, or be prepared to spend significantly more on communications than the established brand. Sometimes, the institutional learning of an established brand gets lost when a new CEO or young brand manager takes over the reigns and ignores, or doesn't understand, the brand's essential connection to its customers. This is the time when hungry competitors pounce.

TRAP

Don't try to tell multiple archetypal stories. Customers have neither the time nor the interest to invest much energy into trying to understand who your brand is. They will, over time, tend to associate established brands with a single archetypal story.

The most effective stories have a main idea or theme. The hardest part for most companies, who want to be everything to their customers, is telling a single story. Just think how hard is it for employees to remember key company strategies. Employees need focus too. If your employees have trouble, just think of your customers. Trying to tell more than one archetypal story confuses both your customers and your employees about who you truly are. It typically leads to telling *no* story, which removes the emotional connection from your communication.

Step 3: What Is Your Brand Promise?

The "brand promise" is what your brand promises to the marketplace, expressed in one or two words. It is different from a tagline in that it is an internal mantra for your employees. This is what your company or brand is offering to the marketplace beyond a product or service. If you are offering them a greeting card, like Hallmark does, what your employees are really offering is "caring shared." If you are Starbucks, you are not just offering coffee, but rather, "rewarding, everyday moments."

When writing your brand promise, start with the noun. What is the one "thing" you are offering to your target. Only after you have chosen the noun, should you modify it with one or two adjectives. Somehow this makes the process much easier. The tendency will be to try to write taglines at this stage.

TRAP

Remember that a brand promise is internal and is not a tagline. A brand promise is your internal mantra—a rallying cry for your employees, your internal secret of success.

While taglines can, and should, change over time as the culture changes and they lose their relevance, a brand promise should timelessly capture what your company really offers besides the products and services it delivers. Your brand promise is your internal secret. Taglines can, and do, change over time to stay relevant to their customer. Internal brand mantras or promises should be timeless.

Step 4: Define Your Brand Essence

Your "brand essence" is what you find at the core of your brand that makes it special and different from other brands. There are different ways of describing your brand essence. Some companies will try to narrow it down to one word. What we have found to be particularly effective is to create a short list of four or five words that describe what your brand is, and four or five corresponding adjectives that describe what your brand is not. For example, a furniture brand chose the brand essence shown in Table 3.3:

Table 3.3. What We Are and Are Not

We ARE	We are NOT
Classic, durable design	Complicated design without function
Integrity	Questionable practices
Personalized-solutions	One size fits all
Enduring relationships	Transaction-focused

A list like the one in Table 3.3 can serve as your guiding light in all your business decisions. It can help you decide what products to launch and what ones not to launch. It can help you understand which advertising campaigns are "on-brand." It can be a powerful tool to help you avoid big branding mistakes. Can you link these adjectives back to the core competencies you defined earlier?

TIP

Try to add definitions and measurements to your brand essence points.

To give this brand essence some meat, try to find a way to measure each one relative to competitor benchmarks. How will you define and measure "classic design," for example? This may require putting new measurements in place. When you look at all the things your company measures, ask yourself if it shouldn't also measure the delivery of your brand's essence. Make sure most of these measures are rooted in the consumer's view of your brand. For example, how do *they* define "classic design"? How do they *rate* your brand on this essence point?

TRAP

Limit the brand essence to five points or less. Employees have a hard time remembering more than this. We have five fingers for a reason.

One company we worked with had come up with 72 traits that defined their brand. Not surprisingly, none of their employees really understood this, nor could they recite more than a handful of traits. Our internal branding needs to be as clear and concise as our external branding. If your employees don't understand the brand, how can they be expected to help your customer understand what it stands for?

Step 5: Define Your Brand Personality

What would your brand be like if it came to life as a person? We relate to brands like we relate to people: we ascribe personality traits to them. The best example of this is the brilliant advertising Apple is doing to differentiate its Macs from PCs. In the commercials, it is defining the Mac's brand personality for you, with great success. We identify with this campaign, because it contains a truth about how we already perceive the Mac and the PC as people. All things being equal, at a crowded party, we tend to gravitate to familiar faces we know and enjoy. Brands are no different.

Write out your company's brand personality. If your company came to life as a person, who would it be? What would he or she be wearing? How would a good friend describe her? What kind of car would she drive? What famous person would embody the personality of your brand? The brand personality is often driven by the personality of the founder, owner, or president of a company, but not always. It is important to define the brand personality for companies that intend to outlast their current founder or president.

It seems to us that Wal-Mart has done a poor job of managing this. Their founder, Sam Walton, drove a pickup truck to work every day, despite being the founder of the world's largest company. After Walton's death in 1992, the company grew to be a dominant retailer and a formidable force with suppliers and communities. Many consumers today do not connect Wal-Mart with the benevolent, likeable Sam Walton. Rather, they view it as a dark dominator. In a sense, for many people, Wal-Mart has drifted from telling the archetypal story of the *regular guy* to the *ruler*.

TRAP

Limit your brand personality description to three or four adjectives. A brand personality shouldn't be a long list of descriptors. Which handful are the most insightful and telling about your company's brand? Which ones are most important in attracting your core customers?

Step 6: Write Your Brand's Worldview

Strong brands stand for something. They either explicitly or implicitly communicate a worldview or belief system that their core customers share. Let's take the Wal-Mart example. For many folks, Wal-Mart has enabled them to raise their standard of living by giving them access to low-priced goods from around the world. Implicitly, there is a belief or worldview here that a *hardworking family deserves a decent standard of living*. This worldview is reflected well in their new tagline—*Save money. Live better.* A competitive retailer, Target, sells much of the exact same merchandise as Wal-Mart does. Yet their worldview would probably be very different. The belief they may share with their "guests," as they call them, might be *cool design isn't just for rich people*. By identifying the worldview that is at the core of your brand, you can better connect emotionally with your customer.

TIP

Try to write your company's worldview. What do you deeply believe in? What belief do you share with your core customer? What did your founder believe in?

Don't make your worldview so vanilla that it loses its punch. A worldview should be both inspirational and somewhat polarizing. A vanilla worldview example might be, "we believe in quality." What is quality? How is it defined? And by the way, who doesn't believe in quality? This is an example of a very internally-oriented view. Try to understand what your core customers deeply believe in and capture this in an inspirational way. It is actually a good thing if it alienates some consumers. This is what will make it connect even more deeply with another group. The Gander Mountain belief we postulated earlier, that hunting promotes strong family values, is a good example of a polarizing worldview.

Step 7: Identify Your Brand's Foundation Story

When you meet somebody at a party, one of the first things you want to learn about them is where they came from. This tells us a lot about who they are. If I meet someone in South Africa and learn they are from Green Bay, Wisconsin, I may start to assume certain things about them. They must love the Packers. They are probably hard working and unpretentious. The same phenomenon is at work when we learn about brands.

Note that we used the words "identify" and not "create." Your foundation story has to be authentic. Find the magic in the origination of your brand or company. Why did the founder create the brand in the first place? What does this story tell us about the brand's reason for being?

In his book, *Primal Branding*, Scott Hanlon makes an important point about the importance of having a foundation story. Nike was founded by Oregon track coach Bill Bowerman, who was constantly searching for ways to help his athletes perform better. In his kitchen at home, he poured rubber into a waffle iron to reduce the weight of the shoe sole by a few ounces, and the waffle-sole was born. So was the company. Nike employees want to know about another company, "What's their waffle?" By this they mean, what is the underlying foundation story that helps me understand what they are all about?

TIP

Write out your company's true foundation story. Give your target an authentic story about why your company was founded in the first place.

What was the core reason the company was founded? Why did the founder start the company? There are many ways to tell a true story. How does your foundation story relate to the emotion your customers are seeking from you today? The emotional lesson employees and customers should take from the foundation story is key. Remember the power of authenticity. Dig deep to find an authentic, true story. At one company we worked for, we discovered that the founder would deliver products by bicycle to his customers come rain or shine. This connected perfectly with the *hero* story the brand was trying to tell.

Today in marketing, you need to tell a true story. Customers and employees see right through a made-up foundation story.

TIP

Always start your branding process below the waterline. This will force you to think hard about what you are emotionally offering your customer and what your brand deeply believes.

You can only tell a true, authentic brand story if you and your employees know the story. If the story isn't true, your employees will be the first ones to see through it. If they don't buy it, how can they be expected to deliver on it?

TRAP

Starting the branding process with the logo. This is perhaps the most common mistake we see. It is caused by a misperception that the brand is the logo, when in truth, the logo is a symbol of all the things the brand stands for.

You've seen this movie before: the company president senses something is wrong with the brand image and immediately calls in a graphic design firm to freshen up the logo. If he doesn't know what the brand stands for, what measuring stick will he have for the design options the design firm brings? If you are a *hero* brand, the celebration of the brand should be bold and courageous. If you are trying to tell an *innocent* brand story, the look will be simple and friendly. Please, define the elements below the waterline first!

Above the Waterline: The Branding Elements Your Customer Experiences

The branding elements above the waterline are cues that customers experience and help them tell the story of your brand to themselves. These elements should reflect the brand story you have defined below the waterline and give clues about the brand in a relevant and differentiated way. Companies that have built strong brands understand the importance of these elements and do a good, consistent job of "telling" the brand story with these cues.

Step 1: Create Your Key Brand Symbols

Every belief system has symbols, which give its followers tangible objects around which their feelings can coalesce. In America, we have a red, white, and blue flag, the bald eagle, and the Statue of Liberty. Canada has its maple leaf flag. Strong brands have symbols too. A strong brand needs its distinct iconography.

The logo is the most tangible symbol for most brands. Think of the golden arches of McDonald's or the ATT globe. A brand's icons need not be limited to visuals. Think of the opening chords of the NFL's Monday Night Football introduction and the emotions these evoke for football fans. Federal Express tells the archetypal brand story of the *hero* by promising to deliver overnight no matter what. Their logo helps tell this story with its bold colors and clever design, which encapsulates a forward arrow in the negative space between the "E" and the "x" in FedEx. Look carefully if you don't see it at first. You will never look at the logo the same way again (see Figure 3.4).

Figure 3.4.

TIP

Identify your brand's key symbols. Use them to tell the brand story or evoke the emotion you want to own. Most brands don't really own more than one or two key icons.

Your customers don't want to have to think deeply about what your symbols mean. The symbols should be easy for them to recognize and identify. The visuals should intuitively lead them to the story. If your brand needs to tell the story of the *innocent*, simple primary colors and rounded shapes might do a better job of suggesting this. A good graphic designer will intuitively understand this. This is why you hire them.

Your brand's iconography can and should go beyond just the visuals. A smell can be a powerful icon (e.g., Johnson's baby powder). A jingle or a sound (e.g., Harley-Davidson), a taste (e.g., Coke), and even a physical feeling (e.g., the Westin Hotel's "Heavenly Bed") are all brand icons.

Step 2: Create Your Brand Language and Tagline

Like countries, strong belief systems have their own special language. If you have ever tried to learn a foreign language in school and then actually use it in the country in which it's spoken, you quickly discover that the actual spoken language is filled with idioms no teacher can teach. There are subtleties you just pick up. In marketing, you want to "speak like a native." Just as a German can easily pick out a tourist struggling with German learned from a book, your customer can tell when you don't really speak their language.

TIP

Understand and be consistent with your brand's language.

The tagline and Web site copy of the brand should be expressed in the brand's unique language. When Nike tells you to "just do it," they are expressing a worldview about the necessity of hard work to achieve your goals. The line suggests a brand personality that is direct and authentic. While not every brand chooses to have a tagline, they all use language to describe their brand. Make sure all your written communication is consistent with this "brand voice." Don't use inauthentic brand language. Be honest. If you say you are the "tightest ship in the shipping business," you had better live up to it.

Step 3: Launch Products and Services That Deliver the Brand Promise

The products you launch and the services you offer help to tell the brand story. Do they make your customer feel the way you want them to feel? Do they build your archetypal story?

When Nokia initially took the cell phone world by storm, Motorola was seen as a stuffy brand. The launch of the RAZR phone helped change this impression to one of modern, creative, and cool. We have found that it is nearly impossible to change your brand image for the better without strong products or services to support the story. Every product Johnson & Johnson launches for babies must be gentle to reinforce the overall caring brand story.

TIP

Describe your product's benefits in a way that is consistent with its brand story.

Consumers buy benefits, not features. The features are there to help them justify why they buy the product. For example, imagine a technology that helps cars better handle steering around curves. If your brand is BMW, you will probably celebrate the handling aspect of this feature, for the ultimate driving experience. If you are Volvo, a brand built on a caregiver archetypal story, you will most likely celebrate the safety benefit of this feature.

TRAP

Launching products that confuse your brand story. Every new product should build on the brand story your customer knows.

It is easy for companies to become enamored with new technologies that offer benefits tangential or even contrary to their brand's core story. If you run into this, ask yourself whether you are not better off launching the technology under a different brand name or even licensing out the technology to preserve you brand story.

Step 4: Find the Rational Alibi

Because they are often not aware of the emotional reasons for choosing a brand, customers need a rational reason. The French-American psychological researcher and marketing consultant Clotaire Rapaille coined the phrase "rational alibi" to describe the excuses we make for doing the things we would probably do anyway. For Volvo, the rational alibi would be the benefit of "safety" when in reality, this alibi allows us to drive a Swedish luxury car without appearing ostentatious. The rational reason for choosing a brand can also be an attribute of the brand. We know Certs as the brand with *Retsyn*. But does anybody really know what Retsyn is (it's a combination of copper gluconate and partially hydrogenated cottonseed oil) or what it does? And yet, it provides a rationale for choosing the brand that its competitors don't have.

TIP

Describe your brand's rational alibi. What reason do they give for choosing your brand over others?

At Johnson & Johnson, the No More Tears formula for baby shampoo was a powerful rational alibi for believing in the gentleness of the product. Create rational alibis that directly support the brand benefit. If your brand is a fresh lemon-scent dishwashing liquid, the lemon-fresh fragrance supports your cleaning benefit. An avocado fragrance probably doesn't.

Step 5: Discover or Create Your Brand Rituals

Strong belief systems all have rituals. Rituals are how we symbolically attempt to reenact things that make us feel the way we want to feel. While we may not think of them as rituals, our daily routine is filled with them, from our morning shower and cup of coffee to our workout routine. Starbuck's understands the ritual experience they provide customers each time they enter the coffee shop and order a latte. When Saturn launched its brand, they created a ritual for the buyer: they would take a Polaroid photograph of the proud new owner and the Saturn employees would cheer her as she drove off.

TIP

Find a way to build rituals into a consumer's interaction with your brand. How can you make the purchase or repurchase into a ritual?

Step 6: Personify Your Brand or Associate It with Exemplary Personalities

The reason many companies seek a celebrity spokesperson is because this is often the fastest way to bring the personification of the brand to life. We all ascribe personality traits to brands, so companies are providing us short-hand for this when they associate their brands with known personalities. Personifications can take many forms, from an actual celebrity or sports figure to animated characters, like Tony the Tiger.

Defining Your Brand—An Example

Let's look at a company that has lived this model well over time to build one of the most respected brands in the world: Johnson & Johnson.

Johnson & Johnson Below the Waterline

1. Emotional need: Feeling cared for or nurtured.

2. Archetypal brand story: Caregiver.

3. Brand promise: Deep, personal trust.

4. Brand essence: Caring.

5. Brand personality: Trustworthy, knowledgeable, warm.

6. Worldview: Johnson & Johnson credo statement, which talks about the priority of responsibilities the company has: 1) to its nurses, doctors, and customers; 2) to its employees; 3) to the communities in which it operates; and 4) to the shareholders (see their Web site: www.jnj.com, for details).

7. Foundation story: The company manufactured bandages for Civil War soldiers, which later became the brand BAND-AID.

The story of caring is implicitly understood by Johnson & Johnson employees. It helped guide the company's behavior through the Tylenol poisoning scare of the early 1990s. The company responded to this crisis the way a caregiver should—by putting the needs and safety of their customers first.

Johnson & Johnson Above the Waterline

1. Key brand symbols: Well-recognized Johnson & Johnson logo.

2. Brand language: Nurture your skin, again.

3. Key products: Johnson's Baby Shampoo, Johnson's Baby Powder.

4. Rational alibi: Many, including "No More Tears" formula.

5. Brand rituals: Bathing the baby each evening.

6. Personification: Association with nurses.

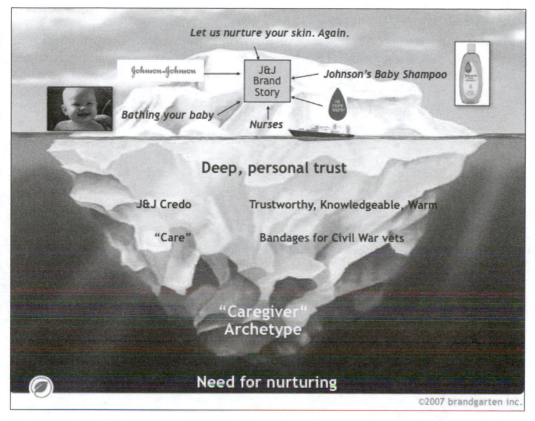

Figure 3.5. Johnson & Johnson's brand iceberg.

This story of caring is told well by Johnson & Johnson. Each piece of communication reinforces the story of caring. In Figure 3.5, you can see this represented in the iceberg brand model. Start at the bottom with the key emotion you want to own. Work your way up to the brand elements above the waterline.

If your brand is telling the *hero* story, the last thing you should ever do is tell the customer directly that you are a *hero*. True heroes would never do this (think Superman!). They just do what needs to be done. Let customers put the brand story together on their own with the cues you give them.

TRAP

Remember that the things below the waterline are for your internal use. The elements below the waterline should guide the development of all the elements above the waterline.

Branding Is Long-Term

Building great brands like Jeep or Johnson & Johnson takes a long time. For many years, these brands have been consistently giving us clues that help tell a consistent story of the *explorer* and the *caregiver*. Don't expect to build a strong brand overnight. The key is to make sure that each dollar you spend on building your brand, and each product you launch, serves to build a consistent brand story over time.

Marketing Planning Model

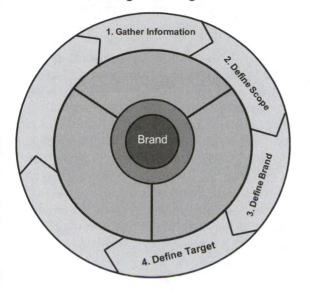

4
Who Is Your Target?

In baiting a mousetrap with cheese, always leave room for the mouse.

—Saki

Who Loves Your Brand?

Just outside of Madison, Wisconsin, there is a small not-for-profit ski hill named Blackhawk. It has three rope tows and five runs of varying difficulty. There is a little warming hut at the top of the hill with a big fireplace and some rustic tables and benches. The club was experiencing financial difficulties, losing money, and unable to retain members. They were frustrated because families would join the club on an annual membership basis, but then leave the club as soon as their kids became teenagers and wanted more challenging runs. Their problem was not that they didn't offer a compelling product or service, it was *targeting*. They were trying to reach all skiers in the area with a broad message, and, as a result, reached very few.

When they asked for our help, we helped them realize that their core target was really *families with small kids learning how to ski*. We helped to reposition them as "a fun place where kids learn to ski" and they started to target families with very young kids. Today, there is a waiting list of 300 to join the club and you can barely find a place to park on a winter Saturday.

Defining Your Target

A target market is a group of people with similar characteristics that result in similar purchasing patterns. It's a known fact that not everyone likes the same things or consumes them in the same way. Take ice cream. Some people like ice cream and others like custard. There are people who are ice cream snobs and only buy premium quality. Some like low-fat ice cream and some don't want to sacrifice any taste at all. There are large families who buy in bulk, for whom quantity is more important than quality. There are individual purchasers who want small containers. There are lovers of ice cream and casual consumers. For many people, ice cream is a comfort food—to be consumed when they need to feel good about themselves. For others, it's a rare treat on a special occasion. Some people only have it when eating out, while others consider it a staple in the freezer.

TRAP

You can't target everyone. A key part of strategy is deciding what you will NOT do. A key part of marketing is deciding whom you will NOT target.

At every organization, the marketing budget is precious. Every penny should work as efficiently as possible to build awareness of and engagement with your brand.

There are many ways to narrow down the target audience. Target markets for consumer products and services, or business-to-business are often determined by some combination of the following:

Demographics

Demographics are factors such as whether you are male or female, your family size, your income level, your age, whether you have kids, and even the geographical area of the country in which you live. Demographics are necessary when you are deciding which media can most efficiently reach your target, but they should never be used alone because they often miss many of the key things that bind a group together.

Attitudes and Opinions

You can also target according to similar attitudes around politics, shopping and purchasing requirements, delivery times, etc. Using attitudes and opinions is one of the most commonly used forms of targeting, but like demographics, they are best used in combination with other factors.

Need States

Mary Minnick, CMO of Coke, describes 10 primal need states that trigger customer purchases of Coke's products. These include things like hunger, thirst, and health. Many food and beverage companies use this approach. This is a broader, more emotional way of understanding your target's needs in a given situation.

Emotional Needs

Targeting based on emotional needs centers around emotional drives such as power, freedom, sexual attraction, caring for others, and the need to belong. Often, individuals can have the same demographic characteristics, but have very different emotional drives for purchasing or using a product. Emotion-based targeting can offer the broadest umbrella that a brand can throw over a target. It is very important for developing succinct, compelling messaging.

Lifestyles

Many target markets are determined by insights into the target's lifestyle. Examples would include the surfer, the athlete, the soccer mom, the outdoorsperson, the single young professional, the country club set, or even the profession, such as doctors, lawyers, and mechanics. Individuals are shaped by the activities and lifestyles in which they engage. The similarities that are formed around beliefs, activities, and life experiences can be used to effectively identify target markets.

Shopping Occasion

Targeting by shopping occasion looks at the reason the individual is shopping —recreational shopping, on a mission, browsing, looking for a gift, looking for a deal, matching an existing outfit, etc. This form of targeting is obviously very important to retailers. Understanding the shopping occasion provides insights into the types of merchandise you'll carry and how to create an effective in-store environment for your customer base.

Type of Company (Standard Industrial Code)

Examples of company type might be finance companies, and, on a more detailed level, banks, savings and loans, credit unions, and brokerage firms. Many business-to-business firms approach targeting this way.

Job Description

This means targeting specific professional titles, such as purchasing agents, senior managers, marketing VPs, or CFOs.

The key is that each of these approaches helps you to define a group of people that will act in a predictable way. Target markets have the same reasons for purchase and similar purchasing patterns. Therefore, you can focus your product, operations, and marketing communications on specifically satisfying your target's needs and wants and in satisfying those better than your competition.

Primary and Secondary Target Markets and Multiple Target Markets

Sometimes you have more than one target market. Many companies create a primary and secondary target market. The primary target market receives most of the focus and budget. However, these businesses recognize that there are other targets that require some attention if they are to be successful.

At Johnson & Johnson, a lot of baby shampoo is used on babies, but a very significant percentage of the volume is also used by dads and moms. Sometimes there is an influencer or gatekeeper group that needs to understand the benefits of the brand. Administrative assistants often control who talks to the main purchasers within a business. These gatekeepers or influencers can be critical to access. Yet the administrative assistant may have a completely different set of criteria than his or her boss. The administrative assistant needs to know how talking to you will benefit the boss. In another example of influencers, kids influence their parents' purchases—just ask McDonald's.

John Deere has two target markets—a current target market and a secondary future target market that will build their brand over the long run. John Deere spends most of its marketing dollars targeting folks who are in the farm implements market today, but they also do a big licensing business in kids' tractors—the future farmers of tomorrow.

One company that has taken a very sophisticated approach to target markets is the electronics retailer Best Buy. Most marketers are very familiar with the *80/20 rule*—80% of your volume comes from 20% of your customers. Best Buy recognized very early that there were certain customers critical to their success, and other customers who were actually a detriment to their profitability. Inspired by the work of Larry Selden and Geoffrey Colvin and by their book, *Angel Customers, Devil Customers*, Best Buy has identified some core customer targets and has subsequently named them:

- *Jill:* A busy suburban mom who wants to enrich her children's lives with technology and entertainment

- *Barry:* An affluent professional who wants the best technology and entertainment experience

- *Ray:* A family man who wants technology to improve his life—a practical adopter of technology and entertainment

- *Buzz:* An active young male, who wants the latest technology and entertainment

(Sources: Best Buy 2004 Annual Meeting slide show; and the *Washington Post, In Retail, Profiling for Profit*, August 17, 2005.)

Best Buy has organized all of its operations around this customer-centric model, customizing its stores to deliver the needs of these targets and training its employees to understand and respond appropriately to each group. For each store, they have determined the primary customer who is likely to shop there. *Jill* is a key target for many stores. In these stores, you will hear James Taylor songs piped in, and the focus of selling will be less on the technical aspects of the products and more on quickly getting *Jill* what she is looking for. When Best Buy runs a commercial on ESPN, their selling message targets *Buzz.*

Best Buy has a huge electronic database supported by Internet purchases with which they built a complex algorithm to help them determine these segments. Your target market efforts do not need to be as sophisticated as this, but the principles can certainly apply. In both cases, you are trying to make your marketing dollar work as hard for you as it possibly can.

TIP

Think target markets first, then consider the segments. It is easy to lose your focus if you start at the segment level.

We just defined target markets as a group of people that have similar characteristics which result in similar purchasing patterns. Segments are smaller groups within the target market that have the characteristic of the target market, but also one or two other similarities that make them unique within the target market.

One example of this is a food ingredient company targeting food companies that create frozen dinners. There may be two segments within the frozen dinner companies—the marketing VPs, who desire innovation, and the purchasing agent, who is looking for value. Both reside within the overall target market of food companies. However, each segment has a slightly different need; these needs must be addressed to make the marketing as effective as possible.

TRAP

Beware of overtargeting and oversegmenting. Don't spread your precious marketing resources too thin to have an impact on any one target.

Keep it simple. Creating target markets (large groups with common purchasing criteria and characteristics) and target market segments (smaller subsets of the target market) can be a powerful marketing tool but it can also quickly confuse a company's focus. Good marketers have a healthy dose of real-world practicality. They simplify rather than complicate. If you can realistically narrow the target down to one group that shares a common need, do it. A common mistake is oversegmenting and, in the end, having too little emphasis on any one segment to make a difference. If a market research firm tells you that you have four key target markets with 11 segments, find another market research firm.

No one has an unlimited budget. Defining the target is perhaps the most critical first step of any marketing department. Whether you have a $3.6 billion advertising budget, like General Motors, or you are a small startup firm, you want every penny you spend on marketing to drive your business goals. To be successful, businesses need to ask themselves, "Where will I get the best return on my marketing spending?" This is not an easy question to answer. Marketing is all about allocating scarce resources. Don't spread yours among too many people or you'll find you're not really talking to anyone.

Marketing doesn't work by trying to be all things to all people. Focus, sacrifice, and be relevant to one group of people or businesses. You should be able to easily define this target description to your internal staff so that they can immediately picture the company's desired customer. The company should easily be able to create actual products and services and to gain access to this target via communications.

Do a great job of creating products, services, and communication for a single target market—and be known and loved by that target—before expanding to another.

Most targeting starts with a hypothesis. Your first hypothesis may not be correct, but it is still best to start with one and then test it. Which group or types of consumers will be most attracted to your brand? There are many ways to build these hypotheses. The first is keen observation. If your product is a consumer product, spend an hour in the store watching which kinds of consumers purchase certain brands. Go online and read the blog chatter on certain brands and categories. If there are big competitors in the category, what kinds of people do they depict in their advertisements? What kinds of messages are they sending, and is there an insight you can take away from their communications? A lot of information is available in the public domain for the observant marketer. If you are selling to businesses, talk to different potential targets that purchase or influence the decision to buy your product.

There are many more sophisticated ways of defining your target. Big companies may choose to do a market segmentation study to identify clusters of consumers who share the same needs and beliefs. With today's technology, it is possible to drill down to very detailed segments of the market—even to individual consumers. This can be a very powerful tool if you are able to customize direct mail or e-mail messages to individuals. David Ogilvy once boasted to a friend that he could write an ad guaranteed to interest his friend. When his friend was skeptical, Ogilvy wrote and ad with a headline: "(Friend's name), this ad is about you."

TIP

For insight into how your company differentiates itself, compare your customer profile to that of the competition and the market.

A quick and easy way to understand how your target market is either the same or different from that of your industry or the competition is to compare your customer profile to your competitors'. In the ski hill example at the beginning of this chapter, the target market of families with young children ended up being very different from that of the competitive ski hills in the surrounding area. As a result, Blackhawk Ski Club developed specific products such as "first flight," through which young skiers could take beginning ski lessons and even ski jumping. The hill hired ski instructors who were skilled in teaching young kids to ski. Marshmallows and roasting sticks became a staple in the warming huts. Everything the ski hill did was directed at being different from the competition. Yes, other ski hills included kids in the make-up of their target market, but only Blackhawk centered its total product and communication around building this particular franchise.

Target market definition must go beyond demographics. More important is how a defined group wants to feel or what common belief system they share. There is a commonly held belief that target markets are more effectively defined by demographics or physical descriptions of companies and the individual titles within the companies than by the use of emotions. This belief is simply wrong. Whether you are marketing to consumers or business-to-business, effective marketers define and understand the motivations behind the core target market that will provide the majority of sales.

Demographics provide an underlying base and a media target, but emotions are powerful separators of what appears to be a large common demographic target market. Al Gore and Rush Limbaugh are both upper-income, highly-educated men over the age of 50, yet their choices of brands will undoubtedly differ. The purchasing agent and the president of a company may both be 48-year-old women, but we're betting they have very different emotional needs based on their positions.

When we purchase a pair of Nike shoes, we certainly want to buy a product that helps us perform as well as we can. The functional benefit of *performance* is important. Yet when we buy Nike, we are also buying the feeling of achievement. When they exhort us to "Just do it," they show us they understand that it is easier to just go back to sleep on those cold, early mornings, rather than getting up, lacing on the shoes, and going for that morning jog. When they tell us "there is no finish line," they are demonstrating that they understand how a jogger feels, even after they have completed a 10K run.

Consider the target of the industrial buyer, a mid-level position that could be further defined by the type of company and the average age, income, and education level of the position. But there's more. There is an emotional insight into this target market. The 8 to 10 hours that an industrial buyer spends slugging things out at the office, trying to demonstrate his value to the organization, trying to work with demanding coworkers, and striving to get promoted to the next level are all emotional insights that provide great texture to the target market description.

Another good example of a business-to-business target market using emotional segmentation is when a plastic thermoform company sells plastic packaging to a cell-phone manufacturer (you know, those packages that are so difficult to open when you get them!). Every day, the salespeople from the thermoforming companies hear the purchasing agents tell them that they need to provide their packaging at a low price with dependable delivery and performance. It would be very easy to conclude that the low-cost provider would win all the business. But this is far from the actual situation.

One plastic thermoforming company we worked with was unsure of whom to target. They considered the marketing executives, the purchasing agents, operations managers, and the packaging engineers. They started with a target market description that included a category of business (cell-phone manufacturer) and position (marketing executives, purchasing agents, etc.). Yet they mined some more—into the emotions of each position—to gain further definition and focus on exactly where to put their marketing effort. After conducting in-depth interviews, they discovered that, while the marketing folks held a high profile within their companies, they were usually not the key decision-makers on packaging issues. They also had a very short tenure at most companies, which meant that there was little opportunity to build lasting relationships with them. It turned out that the operations managers, too, had little influence over the packaging decisions. The purchasing agents played an important role in most decisions but typically deferred decisions on packaging issues to the expertise of the packaging managers, who had long tenures with their companies and were the most receptive to vendor contact.

By narrowing their target down to packaging managers as the key decision-makers, they were able to discover something remarkable. This target was strongly motivated by nonprice factors. They were motivated by a much more emotional need—the need to create and innovate. Within their companies, there was often a very strong drive to innovate faster and better than the competition. The greatest satisfaction they derived from their jobs was when they walked down the aisle of the grocery store with their spouse or kids and could say, "I created that package. Nobody else could do that kind of package, but I did it."

Most plastic thermoform companies did not understand this key insight and continued to compete on the basis of reliability and price, while the company we worked with changed its selling and marketing approach to always lead with its creativity and innovation capabilities. They completely redesigned their trade show presentation, web site, and collateral materials. They even redesigned some elements of their headquarters and signage to better tell the innovation story. Sales went from being flat to growing almost immediately after the first trade show—simply because they had taken the time to better understand the deeper motivations of their targets and to build their marketing story around these insights and core needs of a specific target.

TRAP

Make sure you can deliver the product and service your target market really wants. If there is a disconnect between what your target wants and what you can deliver, your marketing plan will fail.

The landscape is filled with products that failed because no one wanted them. The companies failed to match their target market's wants and needs with what they were actually delivering. If we only examine the automobile category, examples such as Ford's Edsel and the American Motor's Gremlin lasted for only a short time before going the way of the dinosaur. Ford's Taurus was a standard in the industry, but over time became irrelevant and was finally shelved.

TIP

To fully understand what customers love about your product and company, look to the extreme—to the fanatics that are found in your heavy-user customer segment.

Understanding the brand *fanatic* is often the most effective way to provide organizational focus and learning around a given target market. In most businesses, both the category and individual companies have a situation in which the majority of sales come from a minority of customers.

Heavy users should be the first place you look at for defining a target market. While there will be lots of competition for this consumer group, if you build your company, product, and communications to satisfy the heavy user, you will be rewarded in terms of sales volume and profitability. Even if the company doesn't target the industry heavy user, it is important to understand who they are, as this group shapes the competitors' strategies.

Often, the heavy-user target is where the magic of the emotional connection can be discovered. When Ford bought Jaguar, it immediately set to work on the poor reputation the car had for maintenance. But research on heavy users clearly identified that the car was purchased for prestige. Ford could stand for quality but Jaguar lovers wanted panache.

Your heavy users have the most experience with your brand. They also have the most extreme emotional connections. This combination of experience with the brand and the deeper emotional connections make them the perfect research target for learning about your brand. Insights into why they love the brand should form the basis for what you continue to accentuate and communicate over time. Heavy users can offer the window of insight into your brand's appeal.

If you decide on a niche target market, try to dominate that niche. Businesses make a common mistake when they target narrowly and then find that they are faced with multiple competitors in the category, with room for only one, or at most two, to make a profit. If you go after a niche target market, make sure you can dominate the segment.

Today, the Internet can be a powerful tool to aid understanding of your target market. There may be some unexpected niches that can contribute significant volume to your brand. Lego found that many virtual groups were forming online among adult men. For years they ignored this group, until it became too important to ignore. Now the company embraces these grownup Lego fans.

 TRAP

Don't project the belief system of your customers on your noncustomers. Often, they view your company very differently and require a very different marketing approach.

Companies need to work hard to understand the difference between their current customers and their prospective customers. Understanding whether there is a difference in awareness, perceptions, and behavior among new customers and existing customers can be useful to guide strategy. For example, if your current customers absolutely love your brand, but nonusers who share the same needs have never heard of your brand, you have an awareness problem and you will want to focus your marketing resources on building awareness.

Typically, existing-customer efforts focus on increasing loyalty and purchase amounts, while new-customer efforts try to increase knowledge and first trial of the brand. These are very different activities requiring different marketing approaches.

TRAP

Don't overlook the potential of current customers when considering where to focus for growth. Your best prospect is very often your current customer, who knows your brand and would be most open to trying something new from it.

If your current customers are consuming less than the average for your category (purchasing less per order or visit, making fewer visits, etc.), they are the first place to look for growth, because they are already using your services or products. If you have limited resources, it's often easiest to grow your business by focusing on existing customers rather than gaining trials from new ones.

Help All Your Employees Get to Know Your Target Market

So you think you know your target? Great! Now make sure every person in your company does too. Many companies we have worked with try to reduce their target to a single profile. They give this character a name typical of the age, income, education, and emotional attributes of their core target group. Let's call her "Ann." Often, many employees at a company will not have direct contact with their customers. In these cases, their understanding of "Ann" can be the difference between success and failure to deliver the experience she is looking for. At board meetings, they ask: "What would Ann want?" At sales meetings, Ann may come to life in role-playing.

TIP

Bring your key target to life inside your company as a fictional character. Many employees may never have direct contact with the target. Help them understand why your target is attracted to your brand.

How much do you know about *your* Ann? Ask yourself the following questions:

- What does she look like? (find a picture!)
- Where did she grow up?
- What kind of car does she drive?
- Where does she like to go on vacation?
- What kind of music does she listen to?
- What is her favorite movie or TV show?
- Does she have kids? What are their names?
- When she is in the market for your product, how does she want to feel?
- What would she like to hear someone say about her?
- Whom does she admire? Why does she admire this person?
- What is her personality, in a nutshell?
- What are her attitudes toward your brand?
- How does she want to feel when she is shopping your category?

Is Your Target Market Large Enough?

One of the biggest mistakes marketers make is focusing on a target market that is too small and then setting sales and profit objectives that can't possibly be reached.

TRAP

Be careful about choosing a target market that is shrinking over time or that is too small to allow you to meet sales objectives.

A key trait of every target market is that it needs to be large enough so that the company can meet its sales and profit goals. Probably the single biggest targeting mistake is choosing a target market that is too narrow to support your business. Two things could cause this. One, the target is so small it can't support any single business. Or two, the niche target is so small it can only support one or two viable businesses, and there are already five competitors in the category. Three of you won't make it. Before you move forward and set specific business objectives (sales, profit, and marketing objectives), make sure your target market is large enough to get you the sales and growth that you will need to make a profit.

Below are four steps to help you estimate the size and potential of your target market. Use the insights from your findings to consider whether the target market you have defined is large enough to warrant the expectations you have for growth, sales, and profits.

1. Approximate the *total number of customers* there will be in your target market universe. If you are a business-to-business firm and you have narrowly defined one Standard Industrial Code against which you will place primary emphasis (for example, retail firms or construction firms, or service firms, etc.), go to a business list company or the library to determine the number of firms available to you. You might have a size factor or a geographic factor to consider, but it's important to get a fairly accurate estimate as to the number of firms or potential customers. The same would hold true for companies marketing to consumers. Take your target market profile and estimate the total number of potential customers.

2. Next, start considering *constraints* that would reduce the total number of customers in your target market universe. Let's assume you are in real estate. You've chosen first-time homebuyers against which to specialize and build your business with a target of adults 24 to 35 years old. You would further need to reduce the total number of potential consumers by the percent in each geographic location that have purchased a new home in the past two years, as the reality of a repurchase would be minimal within that time frame. In another example, let's assume you are a firm that sells material to construction firms. You've estimated the total number of construction firms in your geographic area. However, your major competitor does business with one builder and has long-standing family ties with them. You need to factor in significant existing relationships and reduce your total potential customer universe based on this knowledge.

3. Calculate the total *potential volume* of the consumers in your target market. With the real estate example above, it would be pretty simple. Estimate the average cost of a house times the average historic percentage of adults who are 24 to 35 years of age who purchase a house each year. For the construction business example, use the average size of a builder's business times the number of builders in your geographic coverage area. For a retailer or consumer goods manufacturer, use the total number of consumers in your trading area times the average number of shopping trips that result in a purchase times the average dollar per purchase.

4. Finally, estimate a rough approximate *market share* your company can reasonably expect to attain and multiply it against the total potential volume from step 3 above. Then, slightly adjust the numbers based on

other extenuating circumstances. For example, if the current housing market is slumping, the construction firm might want to slightly reduce the total estimate.

Keep in mind the purpose of this exercise. You're simply estimating a directional potential for the sustainability of your target market. The figure you come up with will not represent your total sales. Most companies have other target markets. The real estate company in the example above will sell to other customers besides those first-time homebuyers who are 25 to 34 years of age. We would expect that a strong secondary target would be those customers who used the company before and are trading up to another home as their families get larger. The primary target market defines the company. If it went away, the company would probably close its doors. This isn't true of most secondary target markets.

Therefore, use the potential dollar volume of your primary target market as a "red flag" test. It should be large enough to give you a level of comfort so that if you do very well against this defining group of customers, your business will prosper.

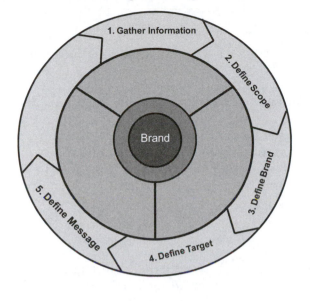

Marketing Planning Model

Brand

1. Gather Information

2. Define Scope

3. Define Brand

4. Define Target

5. Define Message

5
What Is Your Message?

The truth isn't the truth until people believe you, and they can't believe you if they don't know what you're saying, and they can't know what you're saying if they don't listen to you, and they won't listen to you if you're not interesting, and you won't be interesting unless you say things imaginatively, originally, freshly.

—Bill Bernbach

How To Tell Your Brand Story

Once you've defined your brand and target market, it's time to define the message strategy that will tell the story of your brand. Branding is all about how you want your target to feel about your brand over time. It is the big picture story you want them to remember. Every strong brand needs to be differentiated and to stay relevant. Your message strategy is how you achieve this. Every strong brand evokes a set of rational thoughts *and* emotional feelings. Humans rationalize with their brains, but buy with their hearts. The job of marketing is to communicate ideas about your company that strike an emotional cord with your target market. You spread ideas through development of a powerful message strategy that directs all the communication for your brand.

A great message strategy has the following:

1. A *great story* that delivers on a single emotional driver.

2. It answers *seven key questions.*

3. It contains the *words, iconography, and experiences* that help consumers understand the brand story.

Using the above points, the message strategy brief becomes the guide and scorecard for your advertising agency or internal creative department as they develop your communication. Beyond these important functions, it will also guide your sales force, your new product development people, your customer service department, and your operations staff—anyone who helps shape who you are—to tell your story.

Telling Great Stories

Since the beginning of civilized human history, we have been telling stories to guide our groups, connect cultures, and make sense of the world. We understand and remember stories because they are able to deliver an emotional idea within a memorable structure. Every strong brand has an interesting story or it would soon be forgotten. However, we often fail to uncover the real meaning of a brand to the consumer. We try to communicate the science of the brand instead of the heart of a brand.

Strong brands tell great stories that have emotional connections. There are many examples of companies who tell their story around a rational message strategy. We're less expensive. We provide better quality, a wider selection, better materials, the best customer service. Whenever possible, try to connect a rational message strategy to the key emotion your customer seeks when they are choosing your product or service. Faster customer service is a very rational story. All sorts of statistics, like the speed at which the phone is answered or how long it takes to solve an average customer problem are ways companies may try to *prove* this rational story. But when you think about what the benefit of faster customer service really is, you begin to see the emotional benefits that customers get from faster customer service. Imagine the power of telling someone that they won't waste their time in a line or wait endlessly on the phone. We answer your phone call in three seconds, so you can spend more time with your family.

Now which argument is more compelling—we provide consistent ingredients or we don't get in the way of your creativity as a chef?

Volvo cars have a great story. Their brand positioning is around safety. However, the real story, the way to bring the brand to life, is not to simply repeat the word *safety.* There are many potential ways (or message strategies) to communicate safety meaningfully to the consumer. Some are rational, while others are more emotional. For example, here are three potential message strategies or ways into the brand positioning of safety:

1. Better materials and steel (rational message strategy). Convince the target audience that Volvo is safe because of the emphasis on using superior materials and steel, thus producing a safer car.

2. Testimonials (rational and emotional message strategy). Convince the target audience that Volvo is the safest car, because of the many people who have survived crashes and the statistics backing this claim. The message or story is, Volvo can save your life.

3. The parent as caregiver (emotional message strategy). Here, *safety* is what we call the *rational alibi*. It is the rational reason that gives a mom or dad permission to purchase a Swedish luxury car, while still feeling (and appearing to others) like a good parent, who cares about the safety of his or her children. Deep down, the brand connects with parents who want to feel like good caregivers. Using this message strategy, we'd convince the target audience that moms and dads can be better parents by driving the safest car on the market—it's practically their duty!

The G.R.E.A.T. Tips of Storytelling

Remember that a great story has five things in common, the G.R.E.A.T. tips of storytelling.

1. **G**—A great story provides GLUE; connecting our message to what consumers already believe is true; an accepted wisdom. Great stories tie directly to the target market's understanding of the world. Different groups of people have different viewpoints. People have common needs and wants—housing, protection, recognition, hunger, social interaction, to have children and protect them, etc. Yet while there are underlying sets of needs that all people have, there are many different paths that people take to achieve these needs. For example, people of equal incomes don't all drive the same car, drink the same beer, live in the same neighborhoods, or even vote for the same candidates. Marketing needs to explain the differences. To do that, the marketer needs to understand that different segments of people have different values and thus different viewpoints that explain their universe. Some people believe in strong individualism and others that "it takes a village." Some individuals believe that environmentalists help save the world and others that they are misguided obstructionists. Effective stories provide glue and thus an attachment to a specific set of beliefs. A story won't be great unless it is glued to a strongly held set of beliefs that are fundamental to your target market.

2. **R**—A great story provides a REWARD. Great stories promise rewards like sex appeal, weight loss, financial success, better athletic performance,

security, popularity, job advancement, among many others. People always want to know what's in it for them. People will listen if you offer them something that will reward them personally, help their life, or fulfill a dream. Great message strategies help customers see their *best self* in the brand.

3. **E**—A great story connects with EMOTIONS. All great stories appeal to our emotions, not our rational selves. Stories have shaped the history of the world. We believe George Washington was honest, because of the story about his honesty when he was confronted after chopping down the cherry tree. While George Washington may have been honest, the cherry tree story is actually nothing more than a fable. This story about him could be quickly told and remembered. It relied on emotional hooks rather than rational facts. Emotional stories helped shape the brand called The United States of America. They are the key to shaping your brand, too.

   We've all heard the term "elevator story." Emotional stories can be told between the lobby of a hotel and the ninth floor to someone who casually asks, "What's unique about your business?" They are simple, compelling, and are about ideas, not facts. Rather than telling your elevator companion that your company is known for dependability and hard work, you could tell a story about the founder, who started the canning company on a shoestring after his dust bowl parents drove out to California in a flatbed vegetable truck. For the first 10 years, he grew, picked, and canned all the vegetables by hand—never missing a day of work or a promised delivery. Without directly stating the key attributes or benefits of your company, your elevator partner will understand that you work at a company whose people understand the meaning of hard work.

4. **A**—A great story is AUTHENTIC. A great story doesn't have to be totally factual, but it has to be based on the emotional, authentic truth of the brand and the values of the people running the business. Humans get confused with facts, but they remember ideas. The story of Nike as a performance company is authentic, because one of the founders, Bill Bowerman, was the track coach at the University of Oregon and he coached one of the cult track stars of our time, Steve Prefontaine. The story of performance is authentic to the brand.

   Years ago, the brand LA Gear developed as a fashion brand, enjoying tremendous success as a fashion athletic shoe. The shoes were authentic to their name. Then, right at the height of popularity, they contracted one of the greatest basketball players of all time to represent the brand, Kareem Abdul Jabbar. The shoes were making a statement that wasn't at all authentic with their history, the reality of the shoes, or the expectations of their customers. The brand failed in subsequent years only to resurface years later as a low-price brand.

A group of disgruntled IBM employees, who felt there was a better model for computers, started Compaq. Their story is also authentic and also provides a benefit (faster, more entrepreneurial products, and an easier-to-work-with company).

The magazine *Fast Company* was started after the editor of a well-known established business journal toured Japan and became convinced there was a new business model emerging. *Fast Company*'s founders saw a world of collaboration instead of top-down direction, an embracing of technology, and an entrepreneurial spirit that made the typical bureaucratic business obsolete. The editorial content of the magazine was very authentic to the new way of doing business. This insight into the future and the editorial that was consistent to that vision was the basis for one of the most successful new publication launches of our time.

5. **T**—A great story focuses on a specific TARGET audience. To be effective, a great story has to be relevant. To be relevant, direct your stories to a segment of people that share the same attitudes, opinions, and lifestyles. As in all marketing, you can't be all things to all people. Some people like sports, others don't. We've all heard people who tell sports analogies when making a point. This technique is most effective when aimed at a target audience segment that understands and loves sports. This technique is relatively less effective with the target audience segment that doesn't like sports and doesn't understand the references being used.

The Seven-Question Test

You've developed insight into a great story for your brand—one that will best communicate your brand positioning. Now here's a simple exercise that can help you structure your company's thinking about its communication. To help you stay on point and summarize your message strategy, use the seven-question test*—a sequential question and answer exercise that will help you organize your thoughts and effectively communicate your story.

TRAP

Avoid lengthy answers. Each question should be answered with a maximum of five sentences. Get to the point!

---

*Developed by Barry Callen, Emily Child, and Scott Cooper while at The Hiebing Group. Roman G. Hiebing, Scott W. Cooper, *The Successful Marketing Plan*, 3rd edition, New York: McGraw-Hill, 2003.

Think about each word you use and choose words that are from the heart and not of the mind. Use descriptive words that evoke emotions. Use words that you would use every day—at a bar with your friends, at home talking to your spouse or communicating with your kids, or outdoors on a hike with a friend. It's also important to work with other people. Two minds are better than one. The "yes-and" approach works well in this situation. "Yes, that works and this is how I'd add on to your idea."

Developing multiple message strategies is always a good idea. Come at the story from a couple of different ways. You'll be surprised; often you get better and more insightful stories and you get rid of the obvious. You start creating stories that are more unusual but ultimately more important to the target market.

Question 1: Who Are You Talking To?

Take time to describe the customers you want to hear your story. Describe them in detail. This work is directly linked to your earlier target market section. Vague, general statements don't help your creative department or the people creating your communications. We have found that the best way to do this is to actually create a fictional target, based on what you know about the target, as was discussed in the target market chapter (Chapter 4).

TRAP

Don't use business-speak. Use the target market's words, not your own. Use insights into their world.

Question 2: What's the Point?

State the point of the story. Do this in a sentence or two. It's really that simple; ask yourself, "What's the point of this story?" What's not simple is developing a point that is based on emotional customer insights and is the foundation for a moving and memorable story. This section should link to the *emotional* tip in the G.R.E.A.T. storytelling section earlier in this chapter. Which single emotion do you want to own?

Question 3: What's the Key Word?

Can you boil the answers to Question 2 down into one key word? If you only had one word to use as the basis for the direction of your communication, what would that key word be? This is an important exercise. Great communication comes down to *one idea in one ad*. Having the discipline to pick that key word goes a long way to guarantee great communication. For most key points, there are usually several choices. At Johnson & Johnson, we understood that if we owned the word *gentle*, we would own the emotional high ground in the baby care category. The word *gentle* communicated both a functional benefit of the product and an emotional benefit of the brand—"I'm a good parent."

TRAP

Choose the key word very carefully. The sentences you developed in Question 2 will have a number of words that could act as the key word. Review them carefully because each will create a different emphasis and direction in your advertising or creative communication.

Question 4: Why Should I Care?

People need a reason to care. It has to be personal. This is your chance to provide support to your key point. List three to four reasons why your target market would care about your key point and the key word. This provides insight into the rewards that you uncovered in the G.R.E.A.T. tips for storytelling earlier in this chapter.

Question 5: Why Should I Believe You?

This provides the rationale for the key point and key word. It's the proof that the key point is real and *authentic* (as in the tips for G.R.E.A.T. storytelling earlier in this chapter). Some companies call this the "reason to believe." Johnson's Bedtime Bath was one of the most successful baby products to be launched in decades. Emotionally, it helped consumers feel like good parents because it soothed babies before bedtime. The reason they could believe it would calm their babies at bedtime was because the product contained a soothing fragrance of lavender and chamomile—and it was from a trusted brand: Johnson & Johnson.

Question 6: How Should I Feel?

Most message strategies will contain a key insight and tone statement. The tone of the ad may be described as humorous, serious, frank, exaggerated, warm, cold, startling, shocking, expected, etc. This question provides you with the opportunity to spell out how the target audience should feel after seeing or experiencing the communication. The key insight is the "as yet undiscovered" (to the consumer) emotional reason they should choose this product.

TIP

Walk in your customer's shoes. Put the insight in the first person singular. You should write message strategies as if the person with whom you're communicating is actually speaking.

A lot of marketing messages come off as pure puffery. They sound more like what marketers want you to think rather than how you, as a consumer, might really feel. When you make it specific and put the insight in the first person singular, you can ask yourself, "Is this really something our consumer might say?"

Here is an example of a poor insight statement: *"Moms want a healthful, good tasting peanut butter."* Here is an example of a better one: *"I worry about what I pack in my daughter's lunchbox. It has to taste good, but I don't want to give her peanut butter that could be bad for her health."* In the second statement, you feel your target customer's anxiety; as a result, your message can address it.

Question 7: What Do You Want Me To Do?

Every piece of communication should have a measurable outcome. This question provides direction as to what that outcome should be and what you will measure. You might want to increase brand awareness, visits to the Internet site, calls to the company, or purchases of the brand; to change opinions about the brand; or to encourage your customers to tell others about the brand.

For example, *we want to increase brand awareness from 9% to 25% within 12 months.* This way, you will know if you are making progress.

TRAP

Don't make an advertising strategy responsible for more than it can deliver. Prioritize what you want your message strategy to accomplish. Don't expect it to do everything. Message strategies that try to accomplish everything usually end up accomplishing nothing.

So what does a good Seven-Question Test look like? The following example is for Berghoff, a little brewery that prided itself in making craft beer. The insight was that no one knew what craft beer really meant. It sounded scientific. But beer drinkers appreciated microbreweries, of which Berghoff was one, because *micro* meant little, and little meant brewed with care in little batches, and brewed with care meant quality beer. So the GLUE to the target's perception was that *little* meant quality. The REWARD was that quality meant great taste. The tie to AUTHENTIC was that the brewmaster at Berghoff really came from Germany, where the best beers in the world are made. Berghoff had the elements that great stories are made from, the story just needed to be told (see Figure 5.1).

1. **Who Are You Talking To?** 21- to 40-year-old men, who pride themselves on their knowledge of great beers and would rather drink quality than quantity. This is a person who, after the first sip of a beer, sits back and says, "Ahhhh!"
2. **What's the Point?** Berghoff is a little beer, from a little brewery, brewed in little batches, a little at a time. This results in a quality tasting beer.
3. **What's the Key Word?** *Little.*
4. **Why Should I Care?** Because little equals quality, little equals great care, and little captures what microbreweries and craft beers are all about.
5. **Why Should I Believe You?** The beer is handmade from a little brewery in Monroe, a little town in Wisconsin (which isn't that big of a state). Brewmasters, who came from Germany, were making the beer before Wisconsin was even a state. Finally, the brewmaster is a genuine Bavarian brewmaster.

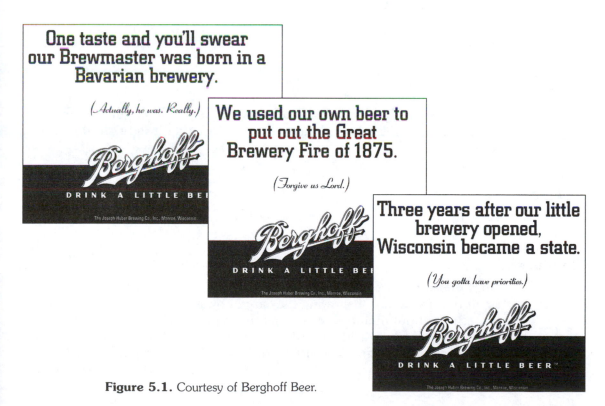

Figure 5.1. Courtesy of Berghoff Beer.

6. **How Should I Feel?** "I know something others don't. I'm in on a secret that few people have. I have discriminating taste."

7. **What Do You Want Me To Do?** Try Berghoff.

Using the Seven-Question Test ensures your company:

1. A common framework. Everyone creating communications is on the same page. You have a vocabulary and a framework for creating and evaluating the creative work.

2. A single method of evaluation. You will quickly determine whether the communication is on message or not. There is one format and one set of criteria for evaluating creative messages.

3. A tight strategy. The tighter the parameters, the more focused the communication. The more focused the communication, the more effective it is in communicating your intended message.

4. A great story based on insights.

How to Use the Seven Question Test

Go back to the G.R.E.A.T. story test. We'll use the Berghoff example in the following answers.

Glue

Does the Seven-Question Test provide the glue to the target market's perceptions? Is the main point based on a target market insight? In this case, it is *quality*.

Reward

Does the Seven-Question Test provide a reward? Yes—*great taste*.

Emotions

Does the story have emotional elements? The target consumers also drink small beers as a way of showing they are knowledgeable and as a way to say something about themselves; i.e., that they *themselves* are not mass produced and are indeed individuals, when compared to Budweiser and Miller drinkers. So the reward is two-fold—the direct benefit of good taste and the more emotional benefit of making a statement about themselves as *unique individuals*.

Authentic

Does the Seven-Question Test provide for an authentic story? In this case, the tie to the *history* and *the Bavarian brewmaster* provide the links to an authentic story.

Target

Is the Seven-Question Test relevant to the target audience? In the Berghoff example, the relevance to the target audience was seen in its ties to the quest for a *small brew* that equaled *quality*.

Here are some final tips for evaluating your message strategy.

- Does the message strategy that evolves from the Seven-Question Test have *legs*? Can you see the communication coming from the message strategy as being long-lived? An idea has legs if, when you hear the message strategy, people around the table start throwing out idea after idea. It becomes contagious and the message strategy sparks many "we could do this" statements. Can you see the communication extending for a long period? Ideas that don't have legs are like one-off jokes that, once told, get old quickly. Look for a message strategy with legs.

- Is the story you're telling believable? Is it something your customer can readily understand and buy into, or is it something that sounds like it was made up by marketers?

- Is the message strategy and story consistent with your brand positioning? Remember, consistency at every point is key to telling a strong brand story.

- Is the story compelling? Does the message grab the target audience's interest and make them want to learn more about the brand?

- Is the message "ownable"? Can you own the story? Is it unique to your product, your company, and your brand, or could just about any other brand in the category tell the same message?

- Is the message differentiating? Does the story set you apart from your competition? Is the story told in a unique and fresh way?

Words, Experiences, and Iconography

You've developed the basis for a great story by coming up with G.R.E.A.T. story foundations, and you've put these into the Seven-Question Test format, which provided you with a succinct message strategy. Now think about key words, rituals, and visuals that will bring your story to life.

Words

Language and words that connect with the target and are unique to brands helps to tell stories consistently and powerfully. Words are important. Think about describing a person. You might say, "He takes chances." However, the words *courageous* or *fearless* conjure up more emotions. So does *risk-taker* or specifics, such as "He cliff-jumps" or "He races dog-sleds in Alaska." In describing a business relationship, you might say, "They're a great partner." But we'd bet that if you would use descriptive phrases, such as "They are good teammates," "They're an advocate for our business," or "They are innovative," you would differentiate them to a much greater degree.

TRAP

Choose your words carefully. Don't use the same descriptions everyone else does. Some words should be banned from the language of branding because they are used so often and are such big tent words that they are almost meaningless, such as "quality" and "solutions."

Most great brands have words that are unique to that brand—almost like an insider code. Think about Starbucks—you order a Short, Tall, Grande, or Venti. Those are very different words than small, medium, large, and extra large. They are unique to the brand Starbucks. "You've got mail" is indelibly connected to AOL. Great presidents and leaders have been defined by their words, such as "I have a dream" and "Ask not what you can do for your country, ask what your country can do for you." McDonald's has a Big Mac, a McChicken, McNuggets, and a whole host of other "Mcs." The brand Apple has iPod, iMac, iBook, iTunes, and the whole iLife package of products that have become words in our everyday lives. "And 1," the basketball shoe, owns the word "streetball."

When you develop your message strategy, think about the words that will define your brand. Start incorporating them into the Seven-Question Test and actually plan to develop unique words that will define your brand in the common language of your consumers.

Experiences

When you order at Starbucks, you order your drink, provide your name, and then move down the counter, where your drink is delivered, your name is called, and you put a sleeve on your drink. This is a big part of the Starbucks experience. An experience is especially powerful when it happens with great frequency (like the Starbucks experience, for their core target). This experience is a little reward I can give myself every day.

The experience for Piperlime, the new online footwear store from The Gap, is all about the way the shoes are presented when they're delivered to your home. This includes the packaging, the coordination of colors (even down to the packing slip), the tissue, and the wording on the card that comes in each shoebox.

Experiences, like words, embed the brand's story in our minds and our hearts. Through repeated interactions, we have certain touch points embedded into our consciousness, and we associate these experiences favorably with the brand. Key words and experiences increase your chance of effectively communicating your story.

Iconography

Symbols of the brands we use are the rallying point for our emotions. We associate the golden arches with McDonald's, the apple with Apple, the swoosh with Nike, the color red with Target, the Clydesdale horses with Budweiser, the mountains with Coors Beer, and the polar bears with Coke . . . the list could go on and on. Iconography helps define brands and makes them stand for something tangible. The visuals help tell the deeper story of the brand without words. These icons can go beyond just the visuals. The smell of Johnson's baby power is iconic for this brand. The jingle for a brand can also be one of its icons.

After you've developed a great story through a Seven-Question Test message strategy, spend time creating words, experiences, and iconography that will help tell your story—through linkages to your brand story that come alive every time you experience them.

Marketing Planning Model

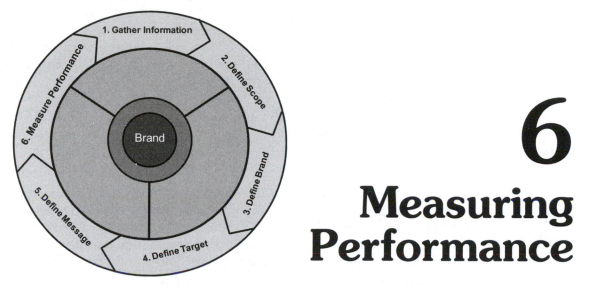

6
Measuring Performance

Set high goals, encourage competition, and then keep score.

—Sam Walton

You Can't Manage What You Can't Measure

You cannot set realistic objectives for marketing your business until you have gathered the right information, defined your brand and messaging, and have a clear understanding of your target. Objectives provide direction to your business. They define *what you are trying to accomplish.* They define what success or accomplishment looks like, through detailed quantification of what you're trying to do.

Most importantly, objectives provide a common language to communicate to everyone in your organization what you intend to do. Well thought out and widely communicated objectives put everyone on the same page. Objectives are the single most important tool you have for getting everyone to work together for the same result. We refer to the objectives in this section as *business* objectives because they are the key things your business needs to accomplish.

If you can't decide what your business objectives are or what needs to be done up front before you start spending money on execution, your business will be using disjointed tactical tools. When this happens, your marketing efforts become inefficient, ineffective, and don't consistently accomplish the things that are critical to the long-term success of your business. When you are very clear on your business objectives, the whole company works toward achieving the brand positioning that assures long-term success, and the sales and profits that assure short-term success.

Your business objectives are the key to profitability. They drive the overall direction and give you the insight into what tactical tools you'll need to focus on in your marketing efforts.

Two separate categories of business objectives are key to the success of your business: *sales* objectives and *marketing* objectives.

- **Marketing objectives** define the outcomes of your target market's behavior. They describe the action you want your target market to perform, which, when achieved, will be directly quantified to a given sales result. The sum of all marketing objectives should equal your total sales objective. Examples of marketing objectives include things such as:

  - Retaining a certain percentage of customers.

  - Getting a certain number of existing customers to purchase more.

  - Gaining a certain number of new customers.

- **Sales and profit objectives** define the sales and profits the company expects to make in a given year. These are the ultimate business objectives against which your performance should be judged. If you don't accomplish your long-run sales and profit objectives, your business will eventually fail or you will be a marginal competitor.

TRAP

Don't set objectives that are not measurable. Make your objectives specific and quantifiable. To effectively manage your marketing function, the organization needs to know without a doubt whether you accomplished your objectives or not. If your objectives aren't specific and quantifiable, this will not be possible.

Good objectives are **SMART** ones:

- **Specific.** Does the objective pertain to a well-defined area?

- **Measurable.** Does the objective have a quantitative measuring stick?

- **Actionable.** Can the objective be acted upon and achieved?

- **Results-oriented.** Is the objective written with the final result in mind?

- **Time-specific.** Does the objective clearly define when it should be achieved?

Marketing Objectives

Marketing objectives should affect consumer behavior and link directly to a sales result. With this in mind, we typically ask our seminar attendees to write three marketing objectives they have used in marketing their businesses on a piece of paper. We then write them on the board for review. Often, we get the following types of responses:

- Be number one!
- Increase awareness of a new or existing product.
- Successfully introduce a new product.
- Expand distribution to increase shelf space for an existing product or a new product.
- Increase sales by 10% with an operating profit increase of 7%.
- Change the pricing to more accurately reflect the improved product.
- Complete the new distribution center and have it operational by year's-end.
- Develop an advertising campaign to change the product's image.

Unfortunately, *not one of these is a marketing objective.* They are all admirable goals and, no doubt need to be accomplished. They just aren't marketing objectives.

TIP

A marketing objective must affect consumer behavior in a way that directly impacts sales. Marketing objectives have a direct consumer behavior link to a sales number.

Each marketing objective should affect a measurable behavior that results in a measurable sales output. Marketing objectives provide you with specific behaviors for which you can develop specific tactics. Marketing objectives also provide you with specific behaviors that you can monitor. If achieved, you'll end up with the sales you wanted to be generated from each behavior.

Marketing objectives fall into one of three categories:*

1. **Retention of existing customers.** If you increase retention of existing customers over the amount that you typically experience, you'll be able to quantify the sales results. You can do this if you know or can estimate the average sales dollars per customer and the number of customers you have at the beginning and at the end of the year.

---

*Roman G. Hiebing, Scott W. Cooper, *The Successful Marketing Plan*, 3rd edition, New York: McGraw Hill, 2003.

Example: Let's assume your business is in the business-to-business category and has 1,000 customers. Each customer spends an average of $10,000 and your business had $10 million in sales last year. Your retention rate is typically 70%, against an industry average of 90%. If the business simply followed its historic retention rate of 70% and didn't pick up any additional customers, sales would shrink to $7,000,000 (1,000 customers × 70% retention × $10,000 per customer).

If your marketing objectives were to *increase retention of existing customers from 70% to 80%, resulting in 800 customers retained,* and you didn't increase the average dollar amount per customer or you didn't pick up any new customers, you could now expect to end up with $8,000,000 in sales (1,000 customers × 80% retention × $10,000). Achieving this marketing objective would result in a $1,000,000 increase over the status quo of 70% retention, all other things being equal.

2. **Increase the purchase amount from existing customers.** Increasing the purchase amount is a customer behavior that also translates to a sales result. You'll need to play with a number of different metrics that are specific to your business. For example, increasing either the number of purchases per year or the dollar amount per purchase provides an increase in the purchase amount.

    Example: Continuing with the example in objective 1, assume you have 1,000 customers at the end of the year and that you will have a retention rate of 80%. Each customer has averaged $10,000 in sales per year. If your marketing objective were to *increase the average dollar per customer by 10% to $11,000 per year,* you would end up with $8,800,000 (1,000 customers × 80% retention × $11,000 per customer). Accomplishing this objective would provide another $800,000 above what you'd expect if you simply accomplished the retention objective in number 1 above.

3. **Increase the number of new customers.** Increasing the number of new customers, or gaining *trial,* also creates sales. Similar to objectives 1 and 2, you'll need to know or approximate the number of customers you have at the end of the year and what they spend per year.

    Example: Assume the business sets a marketing objective of *gaining another 500 customers over the course of the next year.* With the retention rate of 80% from objective 1, there will be 800 existing customers returning. Adding an additional 500 will result in a total of 1,300 customers. With the increase of $1,000 per customer in objective 2, the 1,300 customers will now spend on average $11,000, for a total sales volume of $14,300,000 {[(1,000 customers × 80% retention) + 500 new customers] × $11,000 per customer}. Achieving the objective of gaining new customers would provide another $5,500,000 (500 × $11,000 average spent) above what was accomplished in numbers 1 and 2 above.

Note that each of the three marketing objectives is tied directly to a sales number. Your business may have marketing objectives using each of the three (retention, increase purchase, and increase trial) or simply focus on one or two. In the example, we made things simple by continually assuming that all objectives were cumulative. In the third objective, the new customers were added to the increased retention figure and the total number of customers was applied against the increased dollars spent per customer. Thus, the additive effect of all three marketing objectives would result in $7,300,000 of new sales, for total sales of $14,300,000, or $4,300,000 of incremental sales over the previous year. Table 6.1 summarizes the example provided for each of the three objectives discussed above.

Table 6.1. Examples of the Three Marketing Objectives

	Customers from Last Year End	Customer Retention	Customers Gained in New Year	Average $/Customer	Total Sales
Base Expectations	1,000	70%	—	$10,000	$7,000,000
↓					
Objective #1: Increase retention from 70% to 80%	1,000	**80%**	—	$10,000	$8,000,000
↓					
Objective #2: Increase average $/customer to $11,000	1,000	80%	—	**$11,000**	$8,800,000
↓					
Objective #3: Obtain 500 new customers	1,000	80%	**500**	$11,000	$14,300,000

If none of the three marketing objectives were put into place and implemented successfully, the business would have generated just $7,000,000 in planned sales (1,000 previous year customers with a retention of 70% × $10,000 per customer).

In real life, new customers often account for considerably fewer sales than existing customers. If that's true for your business, you can build this into your *new* trial marketing objective assumptions. Additionally, you may not achieve an increase in dollars spent per customer across all types of customer segments. Again, you can play with the outcomes to obtain expected results that are realistic for your business situation.

Using Marketing Objectives to Manage Your Business

Sales and profits are the key measures of how you're doing in business. You either make your sales and profit goal or you don't. However, total sales, because they are an aggregate number, provide very little insight into what went right or wrong during the year. Additionally, because they are one number, they also provide very little insight into how to manage your business throughout the year. Clear marketing objectives give you the opportunity to manage the relevant pieces of your business during the year and analyze the key components (retention, increased purchases from existing customers, and trial from new customers) at the end of the year.

The following example should clarify this point.

Example Case Study

Sales Objective: Achieve sales of $5,655,000 with a profit before tax percentage of 8%, or $452,400.

Marketing Objective: Maintain retention of customers at an industry-leading rate of 87%.

- Rationale: The company has achieved retention of 87% for the past three years. The historical retention rate, coupled with the phase-in of both the additional sales support in the Call Center and the five-point after-sales maintenance program, will increase the ability to provide industry-leading service and support to the customers. Both the call center and the maintenance program will be unmatched in the industry.

- The company currently has 10,000 customers. The average customer purchases two times per year at $250 per transaction.

- Sales from objective: $4,350,000 (10,000 × 87% retention × 2 purchases × $250).

Marketing Objective: For 50% of the customers, increase the dollar amount per customer by $50 from $250 to $300.

- Rationale: The product upgrade was tested the previous year to great success. If the test results are duplicated, it is very reasonable to assume a 50% success rate at selling the upgrade. Additionally, the new database with its "best-customer" program will allow better ongoing contact with customers and the ability to create incremental upgrade sales opportunities after the initial purchase.

- Sales from objective: 8,700 retained customers $\times$ .50 = 4,350 customers purchasing twice at $300 versus $250. This translates to an additional $435,000.

Marketing Objective: Increase the number of new customers by 20% from the projected 8,700 retained customers to 10,440, or a total of 1,740 new customers. Project new customers to purchase two times per year at $250 without the product upgrade. However, it was assumed that this would be a very conservative estimate given the company's superior after sales service. The expectation was that there would be a significant number of upgrades during the second purchase occasion.

- Rationale: The customer base has been relatively flat the past three years. Even with the high retention rate, the company is seeing declines in its customer base. Therefore, a new customer acquisition program is seen as critical to the long-term success of the company.

- Sales from objective: $870,000.

Year-End Results: The marketing objectives totaled $5,655,000, equal to the total sales objective. Mid-way through the year, it appeared as if the company would not reach its total sales goal. Through superior cost management, by year-end, it met its profit goal. Realizing cost cutting can only work for so long; the company needed to determine why its top line sales fell short. Examining the total sales number does not provide any clue. However, examining the individual marketing objectives would. Upon analyzing each objective, the following was determined:

- The retention goal was exactly on target.
- The increase purchase goal was exceeded by $100,000.
- The new trial goal was short by $400,000. Further analysis showed that the shortfall was dependent on the number of new customers. Additionally, the few new customers the company added spent at the projected one time but did not show interest in the product upgrade.

Now What?

This company explored the reasons for the lack of new trial and found that noncustomer awareness of the company was very poor. The company ranked near the bottom in unaided awareness. Furthermore, the company had poor perceptions among noncustomers of its strength—after-sales customer service. While it thought it had some of the best after-sales service in the industry, it was learning a hard reality—perception equals truth, truth does not equal truth. Customers knew the real story and the company had retention figures to prove it. However, noncustomers, outside their customer base, just didn't know about this benefit.

Since the company's marketing objectives were broken into individual sets of behaviors and each one was translated into a sales result, the company can now manage its next year's efforts by attacking the root of the problem in one specific area, a better communication program. As a result, it will invest more dollars in increasing awareness and educating noncustomers to its strength of after-sales service. More time, more dollars, additional programs, and a company-wide focus can take advantage of this critical area of opportunity. The company can use a rifle instead of a shotgun.

Factors Affecting Marketing Objectives

In the above example, the critical area to manage was new trial. Each of the objectives has a different set of areas that need to be explored and considered. As you manage each marketing objective, the lists in the next section might help you review some of the factors that can act to positively or negatively affect each category of marketing objective.

Factors That Might Inhibit Fulfillment of Objectives

- Retention
  - Product quality
  - Product consistency
  - Product innovation (staying cutting-edge)
  - Customer service
  - After-sales service
  - Perception of brand across critical attributes
  - New competitive offering
  - Poor loyalty due to product parity within your business category
- Increased purchase rates
  - Need for wider range of product options

— Lack of customer loyalty due to product parity within your business category

— Pricing problems/opportunities

— Lack of promotional incentives

— Lack of a competitive loyalty or customer relationship management program

— Lack of add-on purchases

- New trial

  — Lack of awareness

  — Lack of education about product or an understanding of your companies services

  — Product perception and attitudes toward your business or products

TRAP

Don't develop marketing objectives that contradict what you learned in the information-gathering stage.

The knowledge developed in the chapters up to this point should provide a solid rationale for the marketing objectives you've set. For each marketing objective, provide a rationale paragraph that is based on these data and insights. During a presentation, the objectives will answer *what* you're going to do and the rationale will provide the *why*.

TIP

For a reality check, use the insights you gained and the subsequent rationale you developed for your marketing objectives.

For example, if the industry and your major competitors' consumers purchase three times a year and your own customers purchase two times a year, don't suddenly expect your customers to move to 10 purchase occasions per year without some major innovation or change. Use the knowledge you developed to make educated guesses that will prove to be realistic marketing objectives resulting in realistic sales results.

Each business is different from the others in its competitive set and each business faces different situations from year to year. For a couple of years, new trial may be critical. However, you might get to the point at which you have all the customers you can adequately handle given your infrastructure.

Real growth could be realized by getting more from each existing customer. In this case, you might have a couple of objectives against increased purchases. For example:

- Increase the number of yearly purchases from two to three per year.

- Increase the average dollars per purchase from $150 to $175.

Both of these objectives relate to the *increase purchase* objective category. Yet each accomplishes different outcomes and sales results. Your marketing objective decisions will link directly to the tactical tools and marketing activities you choose to implement.

You might find that you've failed in your attempt to gain new customers. Looking back at your information gathering might show that you have low awareness or key areas in which you have to educate customers and change perceptions. If you can't increase awareness, educate noncustomers, and change perceptions, you might never be successful in gaining new trial. This should lead to communication programs designed to accomplish these changes.

Furthermore, a failure to accomplish retention might stem from a poor customer service experience or even a poorly performing or outdated product line. In summary, each marketing objective can be analyzed to discover why you achieved or failed to achieve it and what activities you need to implement in the future to accomplish the specific target market behavior that will build sales.

TRAP

Don't expect all objectives to be equal in terms of the time they take and the emphasis needed to accomplish them. Each objective will provide a different economic value to the organization and will most likely require a different set of strategies and tactics.

Companies that are great marketers don't try to be all things to all people. To paraphrase the book *Animal Farm*—all are equal, but some are more equal than others. Choose wisely and focus. You should prioritize your objectives. If your real problem is customer retention, you might not set a very aggressive goal in terms of an increase in retention, and, thus, the sales expectations from the retention objective will be lower. However, if you've historically achieved a low retention rate relative to the industry or your main competitors, you will need to spend more time in this area to accomplish your goal. Conversely, you may have a new trial marketing objective that brings in a lot of new customers and results in a large sales dollar amount. However, if you've successfully driven new customers into your business in the past and the objective is in line with what you've been historically accomplishing, you may not need to change a lot or put a significant amount of incremental time into this objective beyond what you've done in the past.

Different objectives may need different solutions. Manage each marketing objective separately. There should be different strategies and tactics for each one, as each may require a different set of activities.

For example, say you've retained customers at rates significantly below those of your industry or competition. The strategies and tactics for *retention* could include improvements in your product, an overhaul of your customer service, or more after-sales service. You may decide to create a value-added component to make your product or service more valuable to the customer, or even to develop a faster ordering or delivery process to create a more satisfied customer.

These strategies, and the tactics that come from them, would be vastly different than those needed for gaining more *new customers*. Gaining new customers might involve a change in communications message, additional promotions, a different media mix, or a more robust CRM (customer relationship management or database) program.

At the end of the year, or even mid-year or quarterly, evaluate each marketing objective—separately—to determine your success. You'll probably find that you've accomplished some and you haven't made as much progress against others. In looking at each marketing objective individually, in terms of results, you will be able to manage the various pieces of your business. Individual pieces are much easier and more realistic to manage than trying to manage aggregates.

Sales and Profit Objectives

There are many sophisticated methods for establishing sales objectives. We're going to provide you with two that are very easy to use—a market-based methodology and an internally-based methodology. The market-based approach is tied directly to your marketing objectives, which in turn were driven by consumer insights developed in the *Gathering Information* chapter (Chapter 1). The internally-based method is driven by what you think you need to do to return a fair profit after expenses.

Additionally, you should establish both short-term (one year) and long-term sales objectives (three to five years). It not only helps to know what you're doing this year, but also where you expect it's realistic to go into the future. There will always be a lure to focus only on the short-term, but this can leave you vulnerable to long-term market shifts.

TIP

Once you've determined your sales and profit goals for next year, break the yearly sales and profit goals into monthly and—if your business is volatile—even weekly and daily figures. Make sure to have both sales and profit objectives.

This helps you to know where your business stands throughout the year and also allows you to make mid-year corrections, if you find that you're not on target. Never lose sight of the long-term picture, but understanding the short-term fluctuations will help you better understand the factors that move the market.

Top-line sales and expense control are equally important. But remember, you can only go so long cutting costs before you need to increase demand and top-line sales.

It is a good idea to use more than one method to establish your ultimate sales objective. We provide two different ways to get to sales and profit objectives. Use both and reconcile the two if they are very different.

Sales Objectives: Internally-Based

This method recognizes that in many companies, sales objectives are internally-based and are often established to cover expenses plus provide a proscribed amount of profit.

Internally-Based Sales Projection Method

1. *Determine gross margin percentage:* Look at the historical gross profit margin figures (gross sales less cost of goods sold, returns, and allowances) for your company. Determine if, in the coming year, your gross profit margin will increase, decrease, or stay the same. Project what the gross profit margin will be for the year for which you are projecting sales. *For example, assume that you end at a gross profit margin estimate of 45%.*

2. *Determine operating expense dollars:* Look to your past budgets for a historical perspective of yearly expenses. Now calculate and project next year's operating expenses by budget line and business expense category, such as marketing, administration, etc. *Assume for this example that you end up with $300,000 in expenses* (fixed and variable).

3. *Estimate profit dollars:* Estimate what you need to make in profits after expenses to cover future working capitol and owner/shareholder payouts. *Assume for this example that you need to make $150,000 in pretax profit or 15% of gross sales.*

4. *Project sales dollars:* Add your projected expenses and your profit projection and divide by the projected gross profit margin percentage. *For this example, add your expense figure ($300,000) to your profit figure ($150,000) to get your total projected expenses and profit ($450,000). Now take that total and divide by the gross profit margin percentage to get the projected sales ($450,000/0.45 = $1,000,000).*

The four steps above result in the sales and profit projection in Table 6.2.

Table 6.2. Internally-Based Sales and Profit Projection

$1,000,000	Gross sales
$550,000	55% Cost of goods sold
$450,000	45% Gross profit margin
$300,000	Operating expenses
$150,000	Profit before tax (15% of sales)

This approach shows you how much top-line sales you will need to generate to meet your profitability goals. However, it is only an internal benchmark for what you will need to achieve to stay profitable. It is not a prediction of how consumers will react to your products, services, and marketing activities. For that you need to take the approach in the next section.

Sales Objectives: Market-Based

The purpose of this method is to provide you with a practical, reality-based methodology that directly incorporates the work done in the marketing objective section. The consumer-based methodology detailed below is market-derived, i.e., it comes directly from the work done in choosing target markets, determining their size and potential, and then setting realistic marketing objectives based on behavior goals that tie to a sales number. All the information underlying this work comes directly from insight into customer and consumer behavior as captured in Chapter 1.

Market-Based Sales Projection Method

Simply add up the sales results from each of your marketing objectives. Each marketing objective outlines a measurable behavior that, when achieved, generates a resulting sales number. The total of the sales numbers generated from all of the marketing objectives provides the market-based estimate of your sales objective.

Since each marketing objective ties to a specific sales expectation, this market-based method drives sales objectives directly from the behavior that you expect from your target market. It looks at marketing objectives first and then sums the behavior and expected results to deliver a sales objective.

The sales objective from the case study in the earlier section "Using Marketing Objectives to Manage Your Business" would be:

- Achieve yearly sales of $14,300,000.

Attached to this sales objective would be a subsequent operating profit goal. For example:

- Achieve operating profit of 6.5% before tax or $929,500.

Setting Communication Objectives

Communication objectives define the progress you make toward improving two critical components that affect marketing objectives—*awareness* of and *attitudes* toward your company and products. Communication objectives don't tie directly to sales, as do marketing objectives. However, key measures of a company's ability to be competitive are the awareness and the positive attitudes the company has relative to its competition. Awareness and attitudes are two variables you need to keep improving if you are to increase your sales and profits long-term.

TRAP

Don't confuse marketing and communication objectives. They are very different. Marketing objectives tie behavior to a sales result. Communication objectives affect awareness of and attitudes toward your company and products.

The following are examples of communication objectives that you may use in understanding how to provide communication direction for the marketing of your business. Note: Appendix A provides additional definition and context to the awareness and attitude components discussed in this section.

- Increase first-mention awareness by 1% over the next two years.
- Increase overall unaided awareness by 1% during the following year.
- Increase overall unaided awareness by 2% over the nearest competitor during the following year.
- Increase aided awareness by 2% over the next year.

- Increase specific understanding from 5% to 10% among customers that the business not only sells products but offers a maintenance program for the products it sells.

- Increase understanding that the business provides three levels of products —good, better, and best, providing a product that will give superior value to every kind of customer.

- Increase the perception from 12% to 15% that the business provides an enjoyable shopping experience.

- Increase the perception from 22% to 25% that the business is honest and straightforward in its business dealings, resulting in a partner you can trust.

- Increase the perception from 40% to 45% that the business provides the best value.

Aligning Your Scope, Brand Positioning, Business Objectives, and Communication Objectives

One recent well-known example of a business that didn't connect the strategic pieces of their brand is Wal-Mart. After years as one of the world's most successful businesses, the giant faltered. The retailer momentarily forgot who its target was and why they purchased at its stores. Wal-Mart tried to move upstream and sell clothing that was more fashionable. Within a year of trying to do so, the head of their marketing department was fired, and the company had one of its worst performing years. Known for low prices, Wal-Mart figured it could target the segment of customers that only bought basic generic products at Wal-Mart to do more shopping at the store for apparel. The giant retailer looked at the numbers and saw that certain types of individuals were in their stores, but weren't purchasing what the retailer referred to as "soft goods," or apparel, beyond just the basics. Yet these same people would go to Target and TJ Max to purchase fairly fashionable clothing.

The marketing objectives of cross-selling into other categories could be quantified into a sales result (x% of the customers purchasing cosmetics also purchased apparel, versus y% in the past). The problem was that Wal-Mart didn't first work on changing the perceptions those segments had about the fashion content of their apparel, and they didn't link the marketing objectives to the brand position. The segments that they were trying to affect were satisfied with buying their motor oil, school supplies, and other basics at Wal-Mart, but not their clothing. And certainly not their more fashionable clothing. They believed Wal-Mart all those years as it positioned itself as a low-cost provider of basics. While they were fine with basics in some categories, they weren't about to settle for basics in clothing.

Wal-Mart will recover from its setback. It is one of the world's most sophisticated retailers. However, we use this case to point out the importance of aligning the business scope, the brand positioning, and the communication objectives with the marketing objectives if you intend to achieve your sales and profit goals. We do not suggest that Wal-Mart could have easily changed perceptions. Slight movement of perceptions is possible over time, but for a radical change, you must first radically change the product as well as the communication. Even then, you can't expect quick changes. Wal-Mart provided neither the time nor the major product changes necessary for this to happen effectively. A consumer in the typical Wal-Mart is surrounded by a generic experience and low-price signals, not fashion and trend signals.

Setting good objectives allows you to manage your marketing function. If you follow the methodology we've outlined in this chapter, you will avoid the trap many companies fall into—they know they didn't reach their sales objectives but they can't dissect exactly why. You'll break your marketing into manageable pieces and, even more importantly, you'll be able to precisely allocate your budget to areas that will mean the most for your company's success. Finally, you'll go into the year with reasonable predictions of exactly what you need to do across multiple objectives, based on customer insights. Most importantly, you'll have a good estimate of what sales results you'll achieve for each of the different objectives, the sum of which will total your aggregate sales for the year.

Appendix A, *A Consumer Behavior Framework*, provides a detailed consumer behavior framework for setting marketing and communications objectives. We suggest that you review this material prior to starting work on setting objectives to measure your performance.

Marketing Planning Model

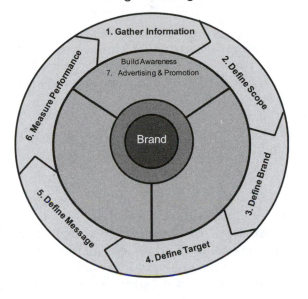

7

Advertising and Promotion

Advertising is salesmanship mass-produced. No one would bother to use advertising if he could talk to all his prospects face-to-face. But he can't.

—Morris Hite

Affecting Awareness and Attitudes

There has been a great deal written lately about advertising being dead. This refers to the massive shift that is currently taking place in the interactive world and the fragmentation of media. There was a time when you could easily reach 30 percent of the U.S. population with one television commercial.

These days, consumers have so many cable choices it is much more difficult to build mass awareness. In addition, many consumers now get their news from the Internet rather than from newspapers, and the power of traditional media channels like television and magazines has diminished. Consumers are able to get much more of the information they want and screen out the information they prefer not to receive. If they are interested in beach volleyball, there are magazines, Web sites, and blogs specifically for their area of interest. In a very real sense, a great deal of media consumption power has been returned to consumers. Marketers are finding new ways to build awareness among their targets, such as product placement and Web-based communities.

There is no question that we are living through a massive restructuring of the advertising landscape. Google now looks like the big winner in the shift from traditional media advertising. YouTube is also emerging as a place where consumers can learn about brands. Facebook has become the communication medium of teens and college students.

However, what has not changed is the need for marketers to build relevant awareness and create shifts in attitudes about their brands among the target groups most likely to buy their products and services.

Building Awareness

The old saying in marketing, "share of mind leads to share of market," is still directionally true. It is extremely rare for a company to have a small share of mind (awareness) relative to its competition and a large market share. You should have at least a "best guess" understanding of how your company ranks in terms of awareness with your target market and the important segments within that market.

TRAP

Don't equate awareness only to the target's ability to remember your brand name. Awareness has an understanding component that's important to recognize.

Awareness has an education component that leads to understanding. Many businesses fail to consider this and thus only look at awareness on one dimension. Our work with AAA exemplified this situation. In the 1990s, the AAA brand name had one of the strongest unaided awareness scores for their category of any brand in America. When people were asked, "What company comes to mind in the roadside assistance category," AAA was consistently on the list and consistently the first mentioned. But AAA had a problem. The organization wasn't understood. Roadside assistance was becoming less of an issue, as automobiles were becoming more dependable, more and more automobile manufacturers were building the capability into their cars, and cell phones were proliferating. The organization had strong renewal rates among members who used the roadside assistance service, but relatively poor renewal among members who didn't use the service. Yet the organization stood for so much more than roadside assistance. It had a marvelous travel agency, insurance offerings, a finance arm, and many other auxiliary services that made the association a very sophisticated travel organization. The problem? People just didn't understand all that AAA could provide. The company hadn't educated its membership about all the advantages of belonging to AAA.

When you think about awareness, consider the relationship between four components:

1. *First-mention unaided awareness.* The percentage of people who name your business *first* when asked what businesses come to mind in your business category.

2. *Unaided awareness.* The percentage of people who, without any prompting, name your business when asked what businesses come to mind in your business category.

3. *Aided awareness.* The percentage of people who, when they are asked what businesses come to mind in your business category, recognize your business after they have been prompted with the name of your business.

4. *Understanding.* The percentage of people who understand the key components of your business and can articulate what business you are in (business scope), your products and services, and why you are different (brand positioning).

Attitudes

Positive attitudes toward a business result in more business and more profitable business. Positive attitudes toward your business are formed by superior performance on attribute rankings critical to your brand positioning. In Chapter 5, we used the example of Berghoff Beer. Berghoff was in the business (business scope) of creating great tasting beer. It answered the question, "How are you different?" by linking the word *little* (little brewery, little batches of beer) to all that little meant, in terms that equated to quality. Therefore, the attributes and perceptions that Berghoff Beer wanted to dominate were around the quality of beer and the connection of the word *little* to the brewery in a positive manner.

TIP

Make sure you are setting communication objectives to change attitudes or further reinforce attitudes that are critical to your business achieving and maximizing its business scope and brand positioning.

Advertising and Promotion

In this book, we define advertising and promotion as communication through mass media—television, radio, the Internet, newspaper, magazines, and outdoor advertising. Most advertising accomplishes one or more of four objectives.

1. Drive traffic to a store, Web site, or office.

2. Increase awareness and knowledge of the company or product in the target market.

3. Increase positive attitudes toward the company or product in the target market.

4. Reduce cognitive dissonance, by reinforcing the customer's feeling after the purchase that he or she has made a good decision.

Advertising and promotion are different tactics, often with different objectives. Advertising typically communicates an idea the company stands for and an image that connects consumers to the brand. Think of some of the great ads and their taglines:

- FedEx: *When it absolutely, positively, has to be there overnight.*
- State Farm: *Like a good neighbor, State Farm is there.*
- United Airlines: *Fly the friendly skies of United.*
- General Electric: *We bring good things to life.*
- Visa: *It's everywhere you want to be.*
- MasterCard: *Priceless.*
- Nissan: *Zoom, zoom, zoom.*
- Bounty: *The quicker picker-upper.*
- Miller: *It's Miller time.*
- Volkswagen: *Drivers wanted.*
- Avis: *We try harder.*
- Nike: *Just do it.*

Without knowing the message strategy or seeing the visuals of the ads, you know what these brands are saying. They have very strong brand messages around the positioning or the differentiating idea for which the company wanted to be known relative to its competition.

With promotion, on the other hand, there is usually an incentive to induce immediate trial or repeat purchase with something other than simply the product or company's concept. Promotions are designed to stimulate short-term sales. Often, this incentive is some monetary offer—a percent discount or a coupon for dollars or cents off the price. Table 7.1 lists promotions you might consider using. Rough response rates are included based on the authors' experience.

Table 7.1. Promotions

Promotion Type	Description	Redemption Rates
Sale	Percent off retail	Varies based on competitive environment and price/quality of product
Direct mail	Printed promotion delivered in the mail	0.5% to 15% depending on the offer
In-product offer	Percent off in product for repeat purchase	3% to 12%
On product offer	Offer flagged on product for future purchase	3% to 15%
Cross-promotion	Coupon on one product for use on another	1% to 5%
FSI (free-standing insert)	FSI with coupon	0.5% to 5%
Magazine	On-page coupon	0.5% to 5%
Refund/rebate	Offer good after purchase	0.5% to 4%
Self-liquidating premium	Product that is offered for the cost of the product	0.5% to 2%
Instant coupon	Offer good immediately	15% to 70%
Newspaper "run of paper"	Coupon in newspaper	0.5% to 3%
E-mail	Coupon delivered to e-mail list	2% to 15%
Rewards	Points or dollars from loyalty programs	15% to 25%

TIP

Set measurable communication objectives for your advertising and promotion. Both advertising and promotion can create awareness, shift attitudes, and drive traffic for sales. Sometimes, they can do all three. Make it clear up front what you expect your advertising to accomplish over time.

Remember that promotional advertising should work right away and affect sales almost immediately. However, brand-building advertising takes time to change awareness, affect attitudes, and result in sales. Be realistic as to your time frame. But don't let the advertising off the hook without setting measurable shifts in awareness, attitudes about your company, and, over the longer-term, traffic and sales.

TRAP

Don't think of the advertising agency or your own creative department as just a group of artists with no firm objectives. Creativity (in product and communications) is one of the few areas left in which a business can differentiate itself.

There's an old saying, "Advertising—done by creative people who don't care about business and approved by business people who don't care about creativity." Don't be fooled. Business people should care about creativity. Creativity moves businesses. Think about it for a second—the most successful companies today, as measured by stock market valuations, are those that are truly differentiated, communicate brand concepts, and don't spend their money buying business through price promotions. Brands such as Apple, the NBA, Nike, Intel, MTV, Target, DSW, Skechers, Smart Cars, and Whole Foods all have creative leaders who take chances, do things differently, and believe in creativity. However, advertising and creativity just to develop an art form is a waste of money. Great creativity and great advertising are rooted in a great strategy.

TRAP

If someone says, "I'll know a great ad when I see it," they're going to cost you a lot of money. Use your message strategy to help you critique the creative ideas and to ensure that you develop effective communications that are "on strategy."

Don't let the decision makers off the hook by letting them say, "I'll know it when I see it." Go back to the message strategy and get agreement. Use the message strategy as a way to judge whether the creative ideas and advertising is on-strategy or off-strategy. The president of the company and the marketing VP should own the strategy. Included in the message strategy is the main point, the tone (how should I feel?), and the focus (what do you want me to do?). The questions in the message strategy provide the box within which those creating the advertising need to play. Argue the message strategy up front. Get agreement and then let the experts in the advertising department decide the best way to communicate the strategy.

TIP

Pay attention to how you evaluate the creative ideas. This is something that few business schools teach, yet a huge percentage of a marketing department's budget goes toward the development and placement of communications. Spend time learning and teaching others in your organization how to effectively evaluate your company's advertising and communications.

When your in-house creative department or advertising agency brings you their ideas for how to build relevant awareness for your brand, they have usually put a lot of creative energy into their ideas. These are their babies. If you call someone's baby ugly, they will most likely get defensive. Creative people are driven by solving challenges that you give them. Try to react to the creative ideas honestly, but with kindness, and if you want change, frame your comment in the form of the *challenge you still want them to solve.*

Here are a few tips for reviewing creative ideas from your agency:

- On the first pass, don't get dragged into the details. Think big picture. You can always work out the small stuff. Big ideas move business.

- Stay open to ideas that are on-strategy but are unexpected.

- Don't review advertising expecting a certain outcome. Be receptive to any idea, especially ones that make you a little uncomfortable. These are often the ideas that get noticed. If they are on-strategy and within the expected tone and sensibilities of the brand, you're much better off with communication that is unique and that people will talk about than with the same old stuff everyone else is doing.

- Be enthusiastic about the work—just as you would if a friend of yours showed you new pictures of their kids.

- Demonstrate your enthusiasm for their efforts and the work by first pointing out things you like. Highlight the best parts of the ads and ask how these can get even more attention.

- Once you've done this, go back and ask questions about things that you don't like. Again, remember to phrase it in the form of a challenge to solve a problem.

- When commenting on creative ideas and advertising, use the "yes-and" technique. For example, "*Yes,* you could use a problem/solution approach *and* you could also focus on our company's long-term commitment to building the health of the community by solving the particular problem of infant mortality." Build on ideas before tearing them down.

- Put yourself in the target market's shoes. Don't be yourself when you judge advertising. As much as possible, be the target market and think with *their* heart and mind.

- Your first, gut reaction is often the best. Don't overthink the advertising. Let the experts work out the specifics.

- Finally, use a checklist to help you evaluate your company's advertising:

  1. Does the advertising meet the Seven-Question message strategy from Chapter 5?

  2. Is there one big idea? Can you easily recognize it?

  3. Will the idea have a long life? Is it easily extendable? Is it easy to think of other ads that will result in a long-term campaign or is this a one-and-out idea?

  4. Will the advertising jump out of the clutter? Is it memorable? Is it fresh?

  5. Is it believable and based on the inherent drama and realism of your company or product?

  6. Will the idea work across different media?

  7. Does the advertising clearly bring the brand to life?

Ideas by themselves are cheap. There are millions of them. Ideas that lead to great communication that is on-strategy are the ones that move a business. The biggest mistake advertisers commit is not viewing advertising as the primary means to communicate their message strategy. Advertising brings strategy to life. It makes it tangible and real to the target market. If you have a great brand concept and a message strategy to tell the story of your brand, hold the advertising accountable for telling that story.

 TIP

When creating advertising and communication, experiment with at least three alternative ways to bring the message strategy to life.

Many times, we get stuck on one idea. It may be the best idea in the world but unless you have other concepts to compare it against you won't know. Additionally, working on multiple ideas allows a cross-fertilization of concepts, by which a second idea is dovetailed into one piece of a campaign and in fact makes the campaign better. Always insist that your creative team develop multiple ways to accomplish the message strategy.

We've found that one of the best ways to develop ideas is to work up outdoor billboards. Even if you're in a business that would never consider using outdoor communication, this medium forces you to communicate an idea in about six or seven words with a single visual idea.

Finally, don't confuse ideas with design. In this day and age, when everyone can design ads on a computer, don't get trapped in developing an ad that looks pretty, but doesn't have a compelling idea.

TRAP

There are no dull products, only dull copywriters. If you feel that your product isn't exciting, you won't get exciting communication.

If you have a successful business that is growing in top line and profits, you have a product that is of interest to a group of people. Every product has intrinsic value and is exciting to the target market that needs it. You wouldn't be in business if this weren't true. The job of the copywriters (i.e., the advertising department) is to find what is meaningful to or excites the people who buy the product.

The screw that goes into the engine provides *reliability*. Maybe the purchasing agent that buys the screws in large quantities feels confident that he or she always gets a fair price, but more importantly, they feel confident that the shipments always get there on time and that any problems will be taken care of immediately. With many such items to purchase, they are buying a worry-free transaction. And maybe, just maybe, that translates into an ability to get away from the office on time and home to responsibilities that are even more important to them than what they do at the office.

A microbrew might act as a badge or a signal that the person drinking it is *not mass-produced* and can make choices that aren't mass-produced. That beer probably isn't about the amount of hops and wheat or brewing process as much as it is about what the beer says about the person drinking it.

There are many established advertising concepts that work. When creating your advertising, consider the following 10 ways to get started:

1. Use a *benefit* approach. Look at the advertising from the end-user's standpoint. What is the benefit of the product to the consumer of your product or service? Midwest Express uses this approach with its "Best Care in the Air" advertising. Consumers can expect the benefit of great care from Midwest.

2. Use a key *attribute* approach. Ford uses this approach with their, "built Ford tough" tagline, highlighting the attribute of strength and durability in their products.

3. Solve a *problem*. One of the most powerful advertising techniques is to solve a paradox. Miller beer did this with their famous, "tastes great less filling" advertising.

4. *Associate* with a winner. Tie into a specific place, person, team, or point in time—anything that is well-known and well-loved, and exemplifies your brand. Coors beer has long associated its beer with the freshness of the Rocky Mountains. Kentucky Fried Chicken built a business associated with a white-haired colonel who made great southern fried chicken.

5. Go directly *against a competitor*. The burger wars resulted in Burger King saying it was better because of flame broiling.

6. Tie to an *emotion*. Find the emotional hook or reason that brings your brand to life. Campbell's "soup is good food" tagline tells parents that they are doing a good job, just like their parents did for them.

7. Capture a *time of year*. Retailers do this with their holiday advertising and other key times of the year for them, like President's Day, Memorial Day, the Fourth of July, "Back To School," and other prominent times in their customers' lives.

8. Become the *user* of your product. Mountain Dew does this by identifying with a certain lifestyle—a young risk-taker—with their "Do the Dew" advertising.

9. *Make fun* of your industry. This technique takes a common industry problem, focuses on it, and then points out that your company has solved it. This technique makes for entertaining advertising that often strikes a point with consumers. AT&T has used this technique effectively with their "dropped call" campaign. The ads focus on things like a call from a boy to a girl he recently met on a date. While he's professing his desire to go on another date, the call gets dropped. The silence causes him to think she is searching for words or clearly is not interested. AT&T is attacking a cell-phone industry problem and communicating that they have fewer problems in this area.

10. Make your product or company name *memorable*. This technique simply focuses on building awareness. Bud Lite did it with their "Got a light" campaign. The sole purpose was to communicate the Bud Lite name, try to preempt the category, and to get consumers to think of Bud Lite whenever they thought about light beer.

There are many techniques advertising agencies use to bring the above concepts to life; Table 7.2 presents some of the most common.

Table 7.2. Advertising Execution Techniques

Use a customer testimonial	Use humor	Answer a question
Use an expert to prove your product's capability	Use a celebrity to represent your product and to communicate who you are	Use slices of life (situations of everyday living)
Develop a music jingle	Create a fantasy	Use animation or cartoons
Tie to a good cause	Provide new news	Demonstrate your product or why it is better
Use an "advertorial" technique (an ad that looks like an informational piece)	Make the ad informational, teach people something	Look "retro" (use of black and white, etc.) to convey that what's old is new or to take people back to a time that says what you want about your brand
Make the promotion the ad	Provide a sample or a guarantee to make it easier to try the product	Use a teaser to get people interested before the main advertising campaign
Provide a premium that says something about your product	Create a character like the Keebler Elves, the Marlboro Man, or the Pillsbury Dough Boy	Use a mnemonic device (or something memorable like a certain sound or a set of unique words)
Create local advertising, tying into local history, people, or places to become part of the community	Become a local or national sponsor and then highlight your support	Provide a percentage off to induce trial
Use the two most powerful words known to advertisers—*free* and *new*—*Grand opening* is also very powerful	Create a memorable or even shocking headline or visual	Create buzz by staging an event or creating a video that will run on alternative media like YouTube
Create a demonstration	Use direct comparisons	Use target insight and speak in the voice of the customer

There are many advertising and promotional secrets to help make your ads more successful. Here are 10 to get you started:

1. *One ad, one idea.* Don't try to make your advertising communicate more than one idea. In our opinion, it just doesn't work. An ad focused on one idea is going to be more effective and memorable than one trying to do everything. If you find yourself trying to communicate two or three ideas in one ad, then stop, go back to your message strategy (see Chapter 5), and rewrite it. Focus on one idea per ad and explode it.

2. *Headlines provide stopping power while copy provides shopping power. You need both to succeed.* Headlines have to stop the prospect with either a believable promise (preferably involving the target market's self-interest) or some intriguing proposition. Consumers in your target market are bombarded with literally thousands of messages each day. You're fighting everyone who communicates for a little share of mind. The headline is your weapon to accomplish this. Ideally, you'll be a miser of words and keep things short and to the point. However, we've found that long headlines with something to say generate more interest than short headlines with nothing to say. Finally, all media have headlines. In television, the headline is at the beginning or end of the spot (television and radio ads are termed *spots*) and sometimes headlines are used in both places in one spot. The same holds true for radio. For direct mail, the headline is the first paragraph, if using a letter style, or a headline and a combination of subheads in a more elaborate printed piece. And don't forget the P.S.—often one of the most read parts of a direct mail piece!

   The work of the body copy is to sell. Often, only around 5 to 15 percent of body copy is read. That's okay. Those that read body copy are very interested and you need to approach them as a salesperson might approach a prospect. If you're actually trying to complete a sale in your ad, you may need to include longer copy. Include as many reasons why a customer would use your product as possible. If they are good ones and each one is different, then keep them. Write long if need be and then edit, edit, and edit some more. If you're trying to sell something, tell people what you want them to do (go to the dealer, take advantage of the sale, buy two items, check out the new models, etc.). Make sure your copy gets to the point. Start with your best benefit and consider repeating it. However, many ads are simply trying to increase awareness or change perception. In these cases, shorter is often more effective.

3. *Simple words are the best.* In his book, *Ogilvy on Advertising,* David Ogilvy provides an example of two ads: "How to Repair Cars" and "How to Fix Cars." The second significantly out-polled the first. Why? In our minds, shops repair things, but people fix things. Fixing sounds like

something you or I can actually do. Repair sounds like it's very expensive and something that you need an expert to accomplish.

4. *Make your ads memorable.* You're in a competition for your target's mind. Ask yourself, is this ad going to be memorable and command the viewer's attention?

   In each ad you produce, make sure something stands out. It can be the visual, the headline, the copy itself, or even white space. Just make sure something dominates. If you have a lot of equal parts, the ad will be easy to miss. This holds true whether you are creating print, outdoor, broadcast, or Internet advertising. Ads without a dominant component may be democratic, but they are also very easy to miss.

   Additionally, the best ads often contain a dominant, focal statement or tagline. As always, think simple—it should be able to fit on a T-shirt. Examples include well known phrases such as "Whassup," "What's In Your Wallet," "Priceless," "Just Do It," "Mm-mm Good," "Tastes Great, Less Filling," etc.

5. *Don't get tired of your advertising.* Advertisers get tired of their ads long before the public does. Wear-out usually follows a pattern. First the marketing director's spouse gets tired of the advertising and then the marketing director does. Sometime after that, the advertising agency tires of the ads. And much later, the consumer target audience gets tired of them.

6. *Avoid multiple type styles in ads.* Keep them as clean as possible. Take a look at newspapers. These guys are pros. They know what works and what does not.

   a. Use serif as opposed to sans serif typeface (serifs are those little angled flourishes that come off of the upper and lower ends of the strokes of a letter—this book is set in a serif typeface). You may notice that this is a very common typeface—it's used in newspapers and other mass consumed print vehicles because it is easier to read.

   b. Type should generally be black on white and not reversed out. Studies show people are used to reading black and white; it's easier on the eyes and therefore it gets more attention. In retail window signing and point of sale use darker colors and light backgrounds for optimum readership.

   c. Photos should have captions that help the reader understand what you want them to take away from the visual. Think of these captions as headlines.

   d. Use a readable type size for your copy. Ad copy that you want to be read should be easy to read. Remember, as eyes get older they require larger type. You should try to go no smaller than 9-point type and, if possible, use 10-point to 12-point type.

e. Keep headlines and visuals from fighting with each other.

7. *Use visuals to intrigue and capture the reader's imagination.* In many instances, readers look first at the visual, then the headline, and finally the body copy. Remember that people read captions of photos and illustrations more than they read the body copy. Photographs provide realism, while illustrations capture fantasy. You can use tints, screens, and special conversions for interest. Color is more interesting to most people than black and white and is often twice as memorable, though in most instances, it's not twice the cost.

8. *Longer broadcast ads are more memorable.* For example, 30-second radio spots cost 70 to 80 percent as much as a full 60-second spot, but a 60-second spot is often twice as memorable as a 30-second spot. The same approximate ratio holds for television's 15-second spots and 30-second spots.

9. *Reality sells.* Consider the reality of the product and service you're selling. There are rational benefits and emotional benefits. Think about each when developing your advertising. Emotional connections are often more powerful than rationale facts. Mothers will be far more attentive to an ad about keeping their child healthy than one filled only with facts about nutrition.

   Bill Bernbach, the famous chairman of BBDO advertising, wrote his 1949 manifesto for the creative revolution and said, "Good taste, good art, and good copy can be good selling." Advertising should surprise and engage without hitting consumers over the head. If the advertising is based on true consumer insights and emotions, it will work much better to convey a business's message. You don't need tricks. Avis created one of the top 100 advertising campaigns of all time by simply delving into the reality that they were the number two rental car company, behind Hertz. They explained why being number two was great for the consumer in their memorable "We Try Harder" campaign.

10. *Find out what your customers want to know.* Put yourself in your customers' shoes. Selling wants is far more powerful and profitable than selling needs. A customer may need new shoes and see them as basic foot covering. But a customer that wants the newest style will pay far more than the customer who simply needs shoes. Find out what the customer wants, the problems that surround him or her getting that want, solve the problems, and provide solutions.

Campaigns provide you a communication platform to develop over time. The best ads are ones that immediately make you think of 10 more ads in the series. Think campaigns, not ads. Examples would be the Culligan Man, United's "Fly the Friendly Skies," Nike's "Just Do It," and many others that stick with one idea and communicate that idea over and over in unique and memorable ways. In summary, campaigns result in one idea being reinforced many times over—a much more effective way to advertise.

TIP

Always try to create a campaign rather than one ad. You know you have a great advertising or communication idea when you can easily think of the next ad and the next and the next. Avoid one-hit-wonders. Brands are built over time and therefore, campaigns, not single ads, build brands.

8

Traditional Media

Today we are beginning to notice that media are not just mechanical gimmicks for creating worlds of illusion, but a new language with unique powers of expression.   —Marshall McLuhan, Father of the Electronic Age

Television, Radio, Newspaper, and Magazines

When we talk of traditional media channels, we are referring to television, radio, newspapers, magazines, outdoor billboards, and direct mail. An old rule of thumb was to spend about 15 to 20 percent of your marketing budget on production of ads (sometimes called your *nonworking* budget), and 80 to 85 percent on actual media impressions on the consumer (your *working* budget). Don't be misled by this rule of thumb to think that the quality of your ads doesn't matter. It would obviously be pretty dumb to spend any media dollars on an ad that doesn't work. However, because the media spending usually makes up such a large portion of the marketing budget, it is critical that every ad reaches as many of your target customers as possible at the right time, so it works as hard as possible for you.

Media planning and buying are fairly technical and require a basic understanding of the components that go into making sound media buying decisions. The purpose of this section will be to provide you with a basic understanding of media best practices.

TRAP

Don't advertise to everyone. Pick a target market and use a rifle, not a shotgun. You'll be more effective.

119

Review your target market. Most media can be targeted by demographics, psychographics, and even lifestyle. Table 8.1 provides a quick reference point for how you can target your media.

Table 8.1. Targeting Your Media

Media	Targeting Ability
Television	Demographic matching primarily by age. Lifestyle segmentation by zip code characteristics (using Prizm, Claritas, Axiom, or similar geo-demo-psychographic tools) to match program content.
Newspapers	Matching newspaper delivery zones to zip code characteristics using newspaper data or firms like Valassis and Newspaper Services of America (NSA).
Magazine	Highly targeted in terms of lifestyle segmentation. Regional geographic targeting also available in some publications.
Outdoor	Matching locations of outdoor to traffic patterns, specific neighborhoods, and locations.
Radio	Targeting through buying according to demographics and matching programs to lifestyle characteristics. Also strong local geographic targeting medium.
Direct Mail	Target businesses, households, and people. Can purchase lists that target business SIC (Standard Industry Code or industry type), business titles at specific locations, or zip codes that match consumer demographics and lifestyles.

TIP

Try to dominate one medium before moving to another. The biggest danger in media spending is not spending enough in a given medium, so your ad gets lost in the competitive noise.

It is important to stand out, and the best way to do this is to have a dominant presence in the given medium, whether it is television, magazines, or radio. This is not to say that you shouldn't try to combine different media. In fact, the most effective media plans typically use a combination of two or three media that reinforce each other with a target. After all, most of your target will regularly *consume* more than one medium.

Media Strengths

Understand the advantages of each medium and determine the best ones for your target market and marketing objectives. Table 8.2 provides a brief discussion of advantages and disadvantages of several media you may be considering.

Table 8.2. Advantages and Disadvantages of Specific Media

Television

Advantages

- Provides both strong reach and frequency against targets.
- Strong creative effectiveness due to combination of sight, sound, and emotion.
- Ability to match content of show with product essence.
- Ability to become part of large, national events like the Super Bowl and the Academy Awards.
- Flexible—national coverage or spot buys, 15-second, 30-second, or longer spots.
- Relatively low cost per point or cost per thousand reached.

Disadvantages

- Expensive in absolute terms because of broad reach.
- Relatively expensive production costs compared to other media.
- Medium is becoming more fragmented.
- Zapping of commercials by consumers.
- Limited ability to finely target by lifestyle against niche target markets.

Radio

Advantages

- Strong listenership during drive times.
- Frequency vehicle—strong ability to get limited audience multiple times with message.
- Strong local medium.
- Ability for value-added to buy with remote broadcasts and station involvement in promotions.
- Strong creative possibilities with theater of the mind.
- Mostly seen as a local spot buying opportunity. However, it is possible to make national buys.
- Relatively inexpensive production costs relative to other mediums.

Disadvantages

- Low ratings per station means it's necessary to make multiple-station buys in order to build reach. Reach builds more slowly than many other media.
- No visual ability.
- Often seen mostly as a more local promotional vehicle versus a medium to build a national brand.

(continues)

Table 8.2. Advantages and Disadvantages of Specific Media *(continued)*

Newspaper

Advantages

- Strong local impact and tie to communities.
- Ability to carry promotional vehicles such as coupons.
- Use of black and white mezzotints and color becoming more sophisticated.
- Strong retail orientation. Consumers depend on it for weekly shopping advice and to see what's in stores and on sale.
- Tabs, circulars, and inserts available to carry promotions and coupon incentives.
- Most papers offer programs of total market coverage that augments direct mail against nonsubscribers, resulting in a greater penetration ability than the newspaper would deliver alone.

Disadvantages

- Limited production quality.
- Low numbers of readers per copy.
- Readership is aging.
- Unlike TV and radio, there are many households that don't get a newspaper. Total reach potential is seldom more than around 50% in most communities, or even less, and declining in most markets.
- Compared to other print vehicles, there is a very short life span for each publication.
- Inserts and Free Standing Inserts (FSIs) are relatively expensive due to both printing and insertion costs.

Magazines

Advantages

- Strong production quality.
- Strong fashion and brand-building vehicle.
- Ability to target segments and niches based on lifestyle and interests.
- Strong pass-along, meaning each magazine is, on average, read by multiple people.
- Ability to provide more in-depth selling and copy due to how the medium is used. More time is spent on average with magazines than the newspaper. They are read on multiple occasions.
- Business-to-business magazines are used for in-depth learning and are highly read.

Disadvantages

- Lower reach than other mass media.
- Not as strong from a local standpoint.
- Requires active involvement, unlike radio and TV.
- Not as strong a promotional vehicle as newspaper or radio.
- Longer lead times necessary.

Table 8.2. Advantages and Disadvantages of Specific Media *(continued)*

Direct Mail

Advantages

- Highly targeted.
- Allows for in-depth copy and salesmanship in print.
- Easily measurable with an ability to match a return on investment (ROI) to each mailing.
- Lead times are fairly short.
- Can carry promotion or coupons.

Disadvantages

- Very costly on a per piece basis.
- Not cost-effective for mass campaigns.
- Increased clutter and a dislike of junk mail by consumers.

Outdoor

Advantages

- Great for quick, simple messages. (Note: words should be held to six or fewer.)
- Can target locations based on driving patterns.
- Strong reach and frequency.
- Strong local orientation.

Disadvantages

- Limited locations.
- No in-depth copy development.
- Typically high total cost per thousand reached.
- Creative limitations.

Geography

Target by geography as well as by your customer target market. Most companies also have a geographic target market that must be considered when developing media tactics. Category development indexes (CDI) and brand development indexes (BDI) are the standard measurements used to help determine geographic target markets. The CDI measures the strength of the product category in a given market relative to all other markets. The BDI measures the strength of the company's brand in a given market relative to other markets. They are calculated as follows:

CDI = percent of category sales in a market/percent of total households in a market.

BDI = percent of company's brand sales in the market/percent of company's total households in the market.

CDI and BDI Example

Let's assume you sell Widgets. If the Chicago metro area accounts for 1% of the total United States population and Chicago sells 2% of all the Widgets, the CDI is 2% divided by 1%, or a *CDI index of 200*.

Similarly, if your company also sells Widgets in the Midwest, and Chicago accounts for 20% of the total households or distribution potential and only 10% of your sales, the BDI would be 10% divided by 20%, or a *BDI index of 50*.

In the above example, the industry does very well in Chicago, or twice the expected average. However, your company does not find Chicago a very strong market relative to other markets that you service.

CDIs and BDIs in themselves do not provide absolute answers. Yet they do provide an easy-to-use reference of both category strength and company strength by geographic market. Once you've calculated CDIs and BDIs using census and industry sources, you can use the information in Table 8.3 to help you think about potential geographic targets.

Table 8.3. Geographic Targeting

Situation	Potential Geographic Spending Strategy
Low BDI/High CDI	Strong market category sales and low company sales—opportunity market, as your company is underperforming in a strong market for the category. Investment spend. *Offensive* opportunity.
Low BDI/Low CDI	Neither the category nor your company do well. *Divest or look elsewhere* to spend money first.
High BDI/ High CDI	Strong category market and strong company market. *Protect* investment and continue to grow market.
High BDI/Low CDI	Strong company market but weak category market. *Defensive* opportunity. Protect what you have but realstically you can only grow the market to a certain point.

Seasonality

Seasonality is another important consideration for your media planning. Most product categories have natural sales patterns that vary by time of year. Accordingly, your company may or may not follow the industry pattern. With this information in mind, you should develop a strategy as to the most productive times of the year to spend money on your media. Similar to the CDI/BDI analysis, you should look to times of the year when the industry and your company does well. If both are strong during specific times of the year, this is a natural time to spend. If your company lags the industry in key selling periods, you should try to spend more to capture increased share, unless there's a compelling reason that you can't do well during these periods.

Understand the seasonality in your category. Gift cards are advertised most heavily during the holiday season. A marketer of watches may spend the entire television budget in the month preceding Christmas. It pays to follow the old marketing adage, "sell salt peanuts while the circus is on."

Also pay attention to the times when your target is most receptive to a message, their *teachable moments*. A common use of this technique is the use of those billboards you see on the highway stating that if you lived in the apartments they advertise, you would be home by now.

TRAP

Don't spend evenly across the year. Dominate the times during which you stand to gain the most. Don't try to spend your way into improving a poor sales period before you've optimized your best selling periods.

A common trap companies fall into is that they think they can easily change customer behavior. It's far easier to take advantage of a trend or a consumer behavior than it is to change a behavior. It's easier to increases sales during periods of the year when you naturally do well than it is to improve the poor performing months.

Famous Footwear, the family shoe store with over 1,000 stores, does very well during the back-to-school period. In fact, this is the number one period for sales, followed by the Easter/Spring break period, with the holidays as the third strongest in terms of sales and profit results. Over the years, the company has found it is much easier, and significantly more profitable, to spend additional media dollars during its number one sales period, back-to-school, than to try to obtain similar results in non-peak periods.

The idea of *flattening* the sales curve hasn't worked for Famous Footwear, just as it doesn't work for most companies. Why? Most companies have natural times of the year that their products, channels of distribution, and customer needs align. Famous Footwear is built for back-to-school, with its youthful product line, its value orientation, and convenient locations in centers that cater to busy parents' need to get in, get out, and get going. However, unlike the back-to-school period, holiday shopping revolves around malls and large box retailers where people can get into the holiday spirit, comparison shop, and get three or four different items in one shopping trip, in one location.

TRAP

Don't just buy media. Learn the media math. Understand the basic principles behind reach and frequency, cost per point, and cost per thousand people reached.

Just because television costs more than radio or one television spot costs more than another, that does not mean it might not be a better medium in which to invest. You need to look at the efficiency of reaching your target. Remember, you're not trying to reach everyone—the real measure is the cost-per-thousand people reached in your target market. Many companies only measure 3+ reach, meaning that they really only care about the percentage of their target they have reached three or more times with their message.

Media Math

Most media is measured against detailed target market demographics and even against lifestyle segments. Let's look at the two broadcast media of television and radio. With both, you purchase GRPs (gross household rating points) or TRPs (target market rating points). A rating point is 1 percent of a target universe.

For example, let's consider Dane County, the home county of Madison, Wisconsin (Table 8.4).

Table 8.4. Demographics of Dane County, Wisconsin

	Male	Female	Total Population
Total	210,020	215,506	425,526
15–24-year-olds	19,203 (9.1%)	18,749 (8.7%)	
5 TRP (5% of the male and female target population)	960 (15–24-year-old males)	937 (15–24-year-old females)	

Let's assume the 10 p.m. news had a 5 TRP against 15–24-year-old males and the 10:30 p.m. rerun of Seinfeld also had a 5 TRP against the same demographic. However, the 10 p.m. news costs $125 per 30-second spot, or $25 cost per point (CPP) ($125 cost/5 rating points) and the Seinfeld show costs $115, or $23 CPP. In the end, each show delivers the same number of people, yet Seinfeld only costs $23 per rating point and the news costs $25. Once you find the ratings and CPP for a number of shows (using an advertising/media agency, or figuring it yourself using Nielsen or Arbitron books or the stations themselves), you'll be able to determine the most efficient broadcast schedule.

Keep in mind that for one week, ads on the Seinfeld show might cost $115, but for the next week they could cost $150. Television and radio time is sold based on supply and demand. If the spots are selling, the cost will go up. If there's plenty of *inventory*, the cost will come down. Additionally, the cost of spots are continually being negotiated. You may start at $25 cost-per-point but end up significantly lower as you go through the negotiating process. The more you know about the trends of the shows over time and the costs of competitive shows, the better you'll do. However, for best results, use an advertising agency or media firm. The CPP can be calculated for every medium, and then the cost per thousand people reached (CPM) can be calculated. In the above example, we saw that the CPP for the 10 p.m. news was $25 ($125/5 rating points = $25 CPP).

The CPM would be calculated as follows:

$125 (unit cost of ad)/960 (size of male 15–24-year-old audience reached with one ad that has a 5 rating or 5% of the total number of 15–24-year-old males) = 0.13.

0.13 × 1,000 = $130 per 1,000 people reached.

TIP

It's better not to advertise and simply put your dollars toward the bottom line, than to underfund your communication.

So how much is enough? To answer this, we need to briefly explore the concept of reach and frequency.

- Percent reach × frequency = GRP or TRP
- Reach is the number of different homes (GRP) or percent of target audience (TRP) that you reach or that are exposed to your ad at least once.
- Frequency is how often, on average, they are exposed to one message.

Therefore, to reach 70 percent of the audience 10 times, you'd need to purchase 700 rating points (70 × 10 = 700). Reach and frequency are normally estimated on a monthly or yearly standpoint but can also be calculated with respect to the length of your advertising campaign.

You may be asking, "Yes, but if I buy 100 rating points of a television spot, will I really reach 100% of the audience one time, or might I reach some households two to three times and some not at all?"

Your media representative can provide you with the exact answer to this question. There are also rating point curve charts that provide directional answers to this question. Table 8.5 provides you with rough estimates you can use. However, we encourage you to find out exactly what your schedule is achieving using the math models your media companies can provide.

This gets even more complex when you are combining media. Again, your media representative is equipped to provide you estimated reach and frequency.

Traditional Media Measurements

A large percentage of your marketing budget will be spent on various media. It is important that you have some common measurements for these media to ensure your spending is reaching its target efficiently. Table 8.5 presents some common measures for traditional media.

Table 8.5. Traditional Media Efficiency Measures

Television:

Ratings based on program viewership and can be found in AC Neilson books. Spot buys provide ratings for designated market areas (DMAs) or local television viewing areas and national buys provide national ratings against the total U.S. population.

Relationship of Reach and Frequency: 100 points of television will give you an approximate reach of 60 and a frequency of 1.7; 500 points of television will provide an approximate reach of 95 and a frequency of 5.3.

Radio:

GRP and TRP Ratings based on viewership per quarter hour and can be found in Arbitron books. Spot buys provide ratings for DMAs or local television viewing areas and national buys provide national ratings against the total U.S. population.

Relationship of Reach and Frequency: Because radio is so fragmented, 100 points of radio across two to four stations will provide somewhere close to a 30 reach and a 3.3 frequency; 500 points of radio will provide a little over a 50 reach with a 10 frequency.

Magazines:

GRP (total circulation divided by total households) or TRP (target readers in geographic area provided by magazine divided by total target readers in geographic area). Many magazines provide an opportunity to purchase regional editions.

Relationship of Reach and Frequency: At first glance, you'd think that this would be very straightforward. If the magazine gets circulated to 25% of the households, you'd have a 25 reach; four ads in four months would get you $25 \times 4 = 100$ points, with a reach of 25 and a frequency of 4. However, remember that magazines have a strong pass-along rate. While the households with the subscriptions will get a frequency of 4, we can't be so sure about the pass-along readers. We can only assume they might be different each month (such as in a dentist's office). Therefore, you have to assume that four magazine insertions in this example would get you greater than 100 points, or close to 150 points, with a reach of 30 and a frequency of 5.

Newspapers:

Similar to magazines—use percent coverage. For example, when calculating GRPs or household rating points, look at total circulation of households. If the newspaper reaches 48% of the households in a given geographic target, your GRP will equal 48.

Relationship of Reach and Frequency: Straightforward with respect to circulation. The number of households or target market reached is the reach figure. The number of ads or days you're in the newspaper is the frequency number. A reach of 40 with four ads would equal 160 points. Note, like magazines, newspapers have some pass-along so you might want to address this similar to the calculation for magazines. However, the concept of pass-along is significantly less with newspapers than it is with magazines.

Direct Mail:

Similar to magazines and newspaper, use percent coverage as the rating point and the number of times mailed as the frequency number. If you mail to the same 25% of your target market two times, you have a reach of 25 and a frequency of 2.

Relationship of Reach and Frequency: Same as newspaper above.

Outdoor:

Usually priced according to a four-week schedule. Similar to magazines, the outdoor companies record circulation numbers that measure the people who pass a given point during a 12-hour period (or an 18-hour period for illuminated sites), including passengers in private cars and public transportation (and walkers). The outdoor company can provide you numbers that translate into a reach and frequency schedule. Like all the other media listed, outdoor can also be calculated on a CPM basis. You essentially multiply the daily effective circulation by the number of days in the showing period and then divide the result by 1,000. Finally, divide the cost per board by this number.

Relationship of Reach and Frequency: Similar to magazine. Some cars will pass by every workday, some very infrequently (similar to pass-along readers for magazines).

Internet:

Number of hits divided by the cost for the advertising equals your circulation or number of impressions.

Relationship of Reach and Frequency: Similar to magazine and outdoor.

So how much is enough? It's generally accepted that for any ad to get into the consciousness of the intended target market, you need to have at least three impressions. This is commonly referred to in the industry as the 3+ or effective reach. It takes more to shift or change attitudes—often two to four times more, and usually advertising alone can't accomplish a complete shift of attitudes around a product. There has to be additional exposure to people who have purchased or experienced the product itself.

You can use the data in Table 8.6 as a rough guideline based on the authors' experience:

Table 8.6. Target Rating Points by Type of Advertising

Type of Advertising	Four-Week Target Rating Points	Yearly Target Rating Points
Brand Building	300–600	1,800–5,000
Promotional	450–900	2,000–7,000

Note that brand building requires a more consistent effort than promotion. This can be done at lower weight levels or spending levels because the objective of branding communication is typically to create positive impressions and build a strong brand image over time. Brand building is not about driving sales during a specific week but creating loyal customers today, tomorrow, and next year. However, promotional communication requires a heavier concentration of media weight and spending over concentrated periods of time. The goal with this type of communication is to quickly build reach and awareness of the promotion and then also include enough frequency to move the consumers to action—all within a short window of time. The biggest mistake a marketer can make with promotional media is to not have enough frequency of message. Also, additional weight is needed during times of new product introduction, grand openings, and during name changes.

TIP

The shorter the time frame you have to achieve results, the more you should spend.

If you have planned a two-week promotion, we'd suggest you start advertising the promotion prior to the start, with the heaviest spending in the first couple of days. We'd also suggest you spend the entire budget within the first 10 days, with the heaviest spending up front.

For longer periods, as in many brand-building or image-building campaigns, you should spread out your spending and consider *flighting*—a media scheduling technique that includes pacing, such as two weeks on, one week off, etc. Pulsing can also be used if you have consistent low levels of media spending or weight with periodic "heavy-up" periods during which you increase the media weights.

TIP

Monitor your advertising to sales ratio (A/S) and your share of voice. Both of these measures provide you insight into the level of media activity compared to your competition.

Through industry sources and your media contacts, monitor your competitors' spending and advertising to sales ratio. Additionally, follow your share of voice ratio (percent of total spending) to the share of voice ratio of your key competitors. Don't expect to steal market share if you are significantly below your competitive set on both ratios. For example, if you have a 7 percent share of voice and two of your competitors have a 15 and a 20 percent share of voice, don't expect to suddenly gain market share.

If you truly have a unique and differentiated product, you'll find that you will be able to profitably increase spending above that of your competition and thus have a higher advertising to sales ratio than is typically found in the industry.

You can also use the advertising to sales ratio to monitor your spending and to make sure you are spending profitably. Since media expenditures are typically the largest percentage of total advertising, the media portion of your budget will be the area of most concern. Through trial and error, determine what advertising to sales ratio is optimal for your company.

Evaluate Your Media Spending

At the end of each year, be sure to conduct a thorough evaluation of your media spending. We suggest two broad areas of analysis:

- *Growth rate of improvement (GRI) analysis:* At the beginning of each campaign or media event, capture the trend in each market in which you plan to communicate. Use at least eight weeks. Capture the market performance both during the campaign or media event and for the eight weeks afterward.

  For example, a market might be trending down at –1 percent growth compared to the previous year. However, during the campaign, the market performed at +5 percent compared to last year, for a GRI of +6. After the campaign, the market performed at a GRI of +2. This means that the campaign boosted sales +6 points during the media buy and that the campaign sustained itself, with a +3 GRI post media spending (–1 trend in versus a +2 post period equals a GRI or growth rate of improvement of +3). Therefore, there was some long-lasting benefit of the spending.

- *Measure against your business objectives, your marketing objectives, and your communication objectives.* Remember, there are many factors that lead to the accomplishment of business and marketing objectives. Your media spending is just one. However, media spending is more closely aligned with the accomplishment of your communication objectives than with your business sales or marketing objectives.

Marketing Planning Model

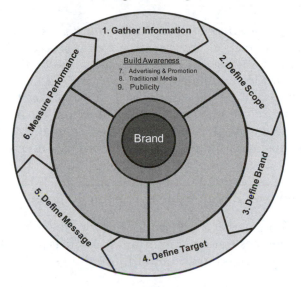

9
Publicity

The caterpillar does all the work and the butterfly gets all the publicity.
—George Carlin, Comedian

Building Your Business with Publicity

You may be surprised to learn that many of the articles you read in magazines and newspapers are not written by journalists. Very often, they are submitted by publicity firms for consideration by the publication. However, if the article is newsworthy, interesting, not overly commercial, and they have space in their publication that issue, they will often print it under their byline. Public relations is often defined as nonpaid communication. But it's much more. It can probably be defined as much by what it's not as by what it is. Here's what it's *not*:

- *Public relations is not free.* Even though much of the public relations effort results in editorial and education through articles, speeches, and personal appearances, the planning and execution time investment is significant and is often more than traditional media.

- *Public relations is not just press releases and news stories.* The discipline revolves around identifying audiences and communicating and educating so that specific goals are met—goals such as raising awareness and understanding, changing attitudes, building relationships, and, ultimately, driving sales.

- *Public relations is not always externally focused.* Many internal audience problems are solved by sophisticated public relations campaigns.

133

- *Public relations is not one-way communication and it's not one dimensional.* Unlike most advertising, public relations involves an ongoing process of communication, listening, responding, and evolving messages. In the end, there needs to be an understanding that isn't always present in advertising. While advertising is often more persuasive in its approach, public relations is focused more on a meeting of the minds and a true understanding between the company and its audiences. Additionally, to effect change and increase positive attitudes, public relations uses everything from events, stories in the press, second-party testimonials, and speeches, to Web sites and ongoing communication programs, while advertising often focuses more on traditional mass communications.

Public relations comprise ongoing activities to ensure that your company has a positive image with the audiences that are important to its success. To have an effective publicity effort, you need to accomplish five things.

1. Evaluate attitudes of various audiences that are important to your company. Determine what they think about you and what is important to them.

2. Develop a plan or a series of policies that will help to align the attitudes and perceptions of the various publics or audiences important to you with your company.

3. Develop communication programs to accomplish step number 2. Determine which forms of communication will be most effective—from news stories, events, Web content, trade show programs, or speeches, to brochures, political involvement, and ongoing educational activities.

4. Develop two-way, ongoing communication that involves talking and communicating with the audiences, listening to their response, and then formulating the next form of feedback and communication. Public relations is an ongoing dance with your most important audiences, a circle of communication.

5. Foster long-term relationships with the key media players and with your public. In the end, the purpose of public relations is to get the media and important influencers to *say good things* about your company— things that over time have become important to you and to your constituencies or various target audiences. Put another way, the purpose of public relations is to get your public to *think good things* about you— things that you want to communicate because they are important to both your company and your public.

Public relations can be broken into the following broad specialties:

- *Consumer influence.* The use of the press, events, and company sponsored nonpaid communication to influence various audiences.

- *Crisis management.* The response of your business to an accident, a product problem, a management problem, or any number of different problems that can cause harm to the long-term image of your company.

- *Cause marketing.* This includes the alignment of your firm with a cause that further strengthens your image by communicating your firm's values and what you stand for in the public arena.

- *Trade communication.* The art of building a positive image within your own trade or industry.

- *Community communication.* The art of building an image and effecting a positive image with the various community consumer audiences (business organizations, civic organizations, civic clubs, etc.) that are important to your company's long-term success.

- *Investor relations.* The art of building an image and effecting a positive image with the various audiences responsible for influencing the price of your company's stock over time.

- *Government relations.* The art of building an image and effecting a positive image with the various audiences inside government that are important to the long-term success of your company.

TRAP

Don't view public relations as just one or two tactics. Publicity is a very broad discipline. Use a combination of tactics to be successful.

When working to change or influence public opinion, consider using a broad mix of the following to do your work:

- Press releases
- News alerts
- Advertorials—paid editorial content, found mostly in print vehicles
- Educational or opinion articles—white papers
- Internal newsletters
- Speeches and seminars
- Web casts
- Editor briefings
- Interviews
- Press kits

- Events
- Brochures
- Mass media
- Internet and Web pages
- Buzz marketing

TRAP

Don't practice spin, practice public relations. And don't wait for the press to come to you—go to them.

Effective public relations will not work if your goal is simply to spin news to fit what you want the world to think about your company. Spin doesn't work; the truth does. You will be much more effective finding things that are true about your company and focusing on those than in trying to put a positive twist on things that don't have a solid foundation in truth.

Be proactive with your public relations. If you don't, someone else will get the coverage you deserve. You wouldn't be in business if you didn't have something very interesting to say to the customers who purchase your products. Most businesses that stay in business have some unique differentiation or innovative products and services. Local, regional, and even national media are always on the lookout for a new story, an innovative product, or a fresh approach to solving problems. Especially in the media world of today, most media sources have fewer resources to investigate stories and are therefore more and more dependent on the information fed to them. Every business has news—a new product, community awards, employee community involvement or achievements, client successes, office moves, leadership stories, articles your staff writes, and public speeches, among many others. You should continually be thinking, "Would this be an interesting story?"

Develop a positive and ongoing relationship with the press. It takes time and consistent work. The coverage you get is every bit as valuable and, in many cases even more valuable, than the paid advertising you purchase because it is perceived as an unbiased endorsement.

It's important to create press releases that are newsworthy. Below are some ways to ensure that your press releases make an impact.

- *Know your audience.* Write your release to one person that represents the audience you are trying to engage. Create content that is relevant and is of great interest to them. Let's say you're an advertising agency and you've been trying to attract companies that target college students. "We're moving to 3411 Commerce Avenue," is not as interesting as, "If you're not part of communicating with the 41 million blogs out there today, you're missing the wave of communication open to businesses. We're moving to 3411 Commerce Avenue because we've opened a new media division specializing in gaming, blogs, and Internet opportunities."

- *Ask yourself, "If I were the audience, would I spend time with this information?"* Whether you liked him or not, Ronald Reagan was great at creating newsworthy content. He knew how to engage his audience by starting his first sentence or two with a problem or a solution that was very important to his audience. Uncover a need and show how to solve it. Focus your release on what's most important to the audience and spend the rest of it supporting your first couple of sentences.

- *Target the reader and the publication.* Create information that is consistent with the publication and that matches its editorial content. Additionally, don't send your press release to "the newsroom" but to a specific person who is most closely tied to your press release's content. Prior to sending your press release, determine the best delivery system to use—fax, e-mail, or hard copy. Finally, follow up your press release with a personal call to see if additional information is needed.

- *Put the words "Press Release" at the top of the page.* Include the date and who is submitting the information.

- *Provide clear and detailed contact information.* Include the contact at your company, your address, phone, fax, e-mail, and Web site. At the end of the press release, include a brief description and background of your company and the industry in which it competes.

- *Give your press release a headline.* Make it a great one. Just like all effective ads, press releases have headlines—your first sentence. Use it to tell the story and grab interest. Often, rushed editors pull only a couple of sentences. It's often the first couple of lines in your release.

- *Address the "five Ws"* (who, what, where, when, and why) *in the first paragraph.* Write in a straightforward style.

- *Keep it simple.* Avoid fancy language, big words, and too many adjectives and adverbs. Also avoid company and industry jargon. You're speaking to a larger audience and this will only confuse them and make it more difficult for them to understand your message. When in France, speak French. Don't speak your language, speak your audience's language, and you'll be more effective.

- *Use facts.* Journalists are trained to ask questions and verify the truth. Including facts will make your press release far more credible and believable. Don't write an ad. Provide information that's based on reality.

- *Include photos and audio or video clips if they are pertinent to the story.* They may not be used, but often their inclusion leads to a larger story than you'd get with written words alone. Adding photos and video also makes the story look larger and more important—again, whether they are used or not, it makes an impression.

- *Consult the Associated Press Style Book and Libel Manual* as a guideline to writing effective news releases.

Figure 9.1 is a sample press release incorporating the above suggestions.

A news release is just one way to engage the press. There are lots of effective ways to get the press interested and educate them about your company or product. If you've got an expert on something of interest, set up appointments and go for a personal visit or press tour. When we were involved with implementing Coors Downtown Beach parties, we came up with a creative way to deliver the press release. We sent guys and girls in swimsuits and flippers with pails containing sand, special back stage passes, an invitation to participate in the tan line contest, and photos of what the event would be like. It worked.

Innovative press packs can be very effective. For example, include small samples. Or, if you run a food company, present your sample in some memorable way—under glass with other special touches from your company, a little information, and a special invitation to sample more at a specific date.

Crisis Management

Don't react when a crisis occurs—plan ahead. Here are a few ways to do that:

- Make sure everyone in your organization knows who will be in charge of three critical areas.
  1. Who will be in charge of gathering and sorting through the information around the crisis and providing the facts?
  2. Who will be in charge of talking to and providing information to the press?
  3. Who will be in charge of the proactive steps needed to solve the crisis?

- When a crisis hits, gather all the information you can as quickly as possible. Talk to different constituencies to get a true picture of what's going on.

- Communicate quickly and in regular intervals. Talk to the outside press but make sure you also talk to those that are most closely affected by the situation. Also, be sure to talk directly to your employees and keep them informed of each new development.

- Above all, be honest. Credible companies retain customers and garner respect from the communities in which they do business.

Press Release

For Immediate Release
NYSE: BWS
Fax, e-mail, and phone here
Brown Shoe Contacts:
Scott W. Cooper or Fritz P. Grutzner
608-442-8222

Brown Shoe Announces Winner of National Student Shoe Design Contest
Winning Student's Design Will Be Produced as Sample Shoe

ST. LOUIS, March 20, 2006 — A panel of designers, editors and fashion industry luminaries chose Parsons School of Design student Joo-Huyn Lee as the winner of the first Brown Shoe Student Shoe Design Contest, which solicited original shoe designs from college students majoring in fashion, design, or a related field.

Brown Shoe Company, Inc. (NYSE: BWS, www.brownshoe.com) launched the Student Shoe Design Contest in 2005 to recognize emerging talent in the footwear industry. Lee, who is currently pursuing her Associated Applied Science degree in fashion design, submitted sketches of men's and women's ankle boots and women's flats to the competition.

"I've always been interested in fashion accessories, especially shoes. Shoes are the most important element of fashion," said Lee. "I wasn't sure about my future, what I wanted to do, what I wanted to be. The one thing I knew is that I wanted to use my hands—fashion illustration, drawing. But now, I know I want to be a shoe designer."

The entries were culled down to two finalists, who then submitted a second round of drawings for review. A panel of judges, including designer and talk show host Isaac Mizrahi, *Elle* magazine creative director Gilles Bensimon, *InStyle* magazine's accessories editor Alice Kim, *Footwear News* magazine's fashion director Jennifer Mooney, and Brown Shoe's vice president of product development Rick Gelber, selected Lee's designs to win.

"I liked her design aesthetic," said Kim. "It was modern, sophisticated with clean lines but with some link to the past, creating a somewhat vintage approach to design."

One of Lee's shoes will be put into the production process, and a sample will be made. She also received a cash prize of $5,000, and attended the World Shoe Association's Las Vegas shoe show in February as Brown Shoe's guest.

"Recognizing emerging designers is an important commitment for the entire footwear industry," said Gelber. "This contest provides invaluable, real world experience for students, and helps make the industry aware of rising talent . . . which just might lead to finding the next legendary shoe designer."

Brown Shoe is a $2.3 billion footwear company with global operations. The Company operates the 900+ store Famous Footwear chain, which sells *brand name shoes for the family*. It also operates 300+ specialty retail stores in the U.S. and Canada under the Naturalizer, FX LaSalle, and Via Spiga names, and Shoes.com, the Company's e-commerce subsidiary. Brown Shoe, through its Wholesale divisions, owns and markets leading footwear brands, including Naturalizer, LifeStride, Via Spiga, Nickels Soft, Connie, and Buster Brown; it also markets licensed brands, including Franco Sarto, Dr. Scholl's, Etienne Aigner, Bass, and Carlos by Carlos Santana for adults, and Barbie, Disney, and Nickelodeon character footwear for children. Brown Shoe press releases are available on the Company's Web site at www.brownshoe.com.

Figure 9.1. Sample press release from Brown Shoe.

Trade Shows and Events

For business-to-business firms, trade shows can be one of the most efficient ways of marketing your business. They attract a large audience already interested in the products or services you are selling. A good trade show plan should include preshow activities, the development of sound objectives to be met during the show, and a strong postshow program.

Trade show costs can get out of control—make sure you're maximizing your expenditures as you would with any other advertising or marketing.

- *Ask for the percentage of participants that match your target market.* If it's a trade show for marketing executives, make sure you ask for the job title that's most responsible for the purchase or influence on the purchase of your product. For example, the media manager, the Internet director, the VP of strategic planning, etc.

- *Take advantage of the marketing value-adds that are available with most trade shows.* Many allow access to mailing lists and attendees names and addresses including e-mail. This allows for pre- and postshow communication as well as preparation for specific booth content. Many trade shows also have preshow shows, and postshow publications. Also, most shows have forums with speakers. These provide excellent visibility for those selected to participate.

- *Spend money to be where the action is in the convention center.* Your location says a lot about your brand, so the placement of your booth matters. If the show groups similar vendors together and you don't like where your classification is located, there are many creative alternatives you can explore. Ask to partner with a larger vendor or one that's in a more desirable location. Provide preshow incentives or a reason to make the trip to your booth. You're already spending good money to be part of the show, now work hard to make your time as effective as possible.

- *On the flip side of the above point, there are ways to spend less money.* First, ask for a discount. You'd be surprised how many shows will provide one. They want vendors and your presence is valued. Or, reduce the size of your booth, but explore ways to increase the impact.

  Sonic Foundry was a small software company that had a revolutionary new product called ACID. ACID allowed just about anyone to sit down and compose music. Sonic Foundry wanted to make a splash at COMDEX, which is one of the biggest trade shows in the world, and is attended by all the big names in the software and computer industry. So we developed the ultimate street fighting campaign:

  — When trade attendees got off the plane in the Las Vegas airport, they were greeted with protesters (hired actors) deploring ACID, with sayings like, "Acid, the end of music as we know it—don't go to booth 4590."

— When the attendees got to the luggage carousel, they saw hundreds of guitar cases going around and around, with various messages like "ACID, play the toot toot old man." "ACID, screw muskrat love." "ACID, louder than Vegas."

— On the way to the hotel, more "protesters."

— All the buses in Vegas had more of the billboard sayings that attendees had seen in the airport.

— Men's restrooms had urinal cakes saying, "ACID, Beethoven's pissed."

— Live demonstrations at the Sonic Foundry booth were interrupted by periodic police raids, with officers (hired actors) coming in and shutting down the booth.

The result—publicity in national publications, including both general interest publications and many leading software and industry publications, buy-in of the product from most leading big-box retailers, a rapid rise in the stock price, and the COMDEX Marketer of the Year award.

TIP

When considering events or live marketing, make sure you have a set objective you want to accomplish. They can be used to sample your product, raise awareness, educate and inform, provide an experience with your product to increase customer connection to your brand, increase continuity of purchase, help position your product, recruit new employees, celebrate the grand opening of a new store, gain publicity, or help change attitudes.

Marketing Planning Model

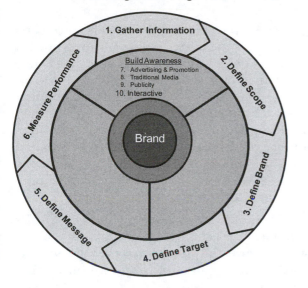

10
Interactive Marketing

We can't expect consumers to come to us. It's arrogant for any media company to assume that.
—Quincy Smith, President, CBS Interactive

New Media for a New Age

The Internet. It's the fastest growing communication tool we have today. Over 70 percent of U.S. citizens now use the Internet. Online sales have grown to over $146 billion in 2006. Predictions for 2007 have online sales increasing another 19 percent in 2007 to $174.5 billion, with similar growth expected through 2012.

As the Internet grows, so does the sophistication of Internet marketing among businesses of all sizes. The low cost of Internet marketing is particularly advantageous for small businesses. Because of the relatively low cost of acquisition and retention of customers and ease of tracking results, Internet marketing is one of the few areas in which a small business can compete on a level playing field with competitors who are much larger and better financed.

Typically, when businesses discuss Internet marketing, there are five activity categories in which they may be engaged.

1. *Generating sales for products and services.* A successful Internet marketing program will increase your company's sales by expanding your consumer base, increasing the availability of information, and maximizing consumer traffic. For many products and services, it is appropriate to sell directly from your Web site.

143

2. *Pre-shopping and generating leads.* A large use of the Internet is for research and pre-shopping. This is certainly true in business-to-business and services marketing, and it's also very common in consumer marketing. Sites such as www.chevrolet.com allow customers to see current special offers, search for and compare cars, explore different financing options, request information, and search for nearby Chevy dealers. The transaction isn't completed until the customer goes to a physical location. Retailers like Famous Footwear report that over half the visitors to their Web site use it to pre-shop prior to coming into Famous Footwear. Accordingly, Forrester Research reports that the Internet is used more for pre-shopping than for actual purchasing.

3. *Complementing other media and brand communications.* The Dove® mass media campaign took a unique approach by acknowledging the beauty in all women and all body types. Dove, the global beauty brand, launched the Campaign For Real Beauty to support the Dove mission to make more women feel beautiful every day by widening stereotypical views of beauty. The Dove Web site, www.campaignforrealbeauty.com (Figure 10.1), complements the campaign by providing a forum in which men and women are encouraged to share their views on beauty. The site

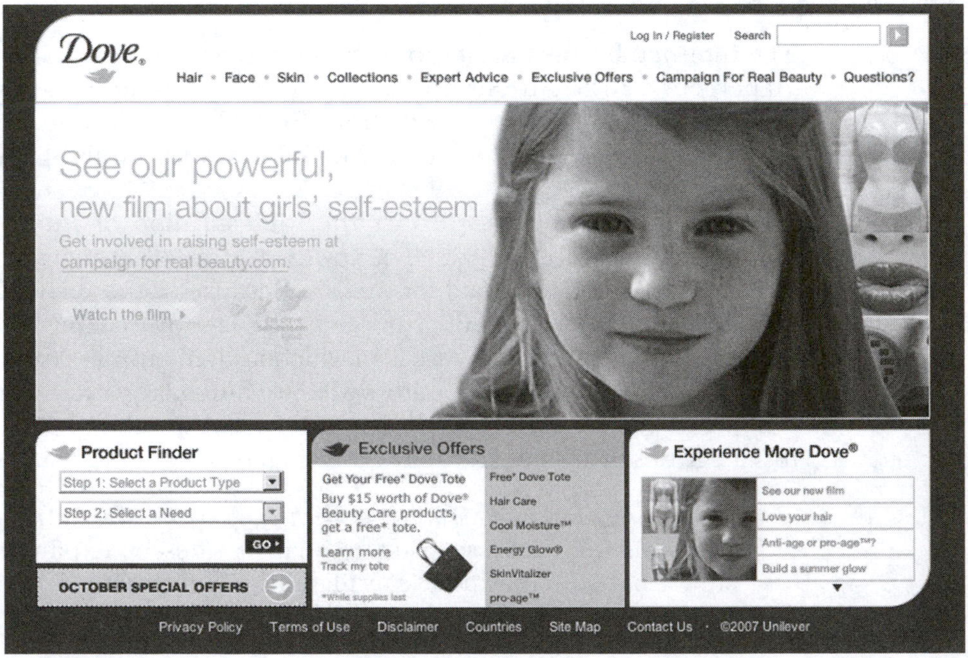

Figure 10.1. This Dove Web site complements offline efforts and reinforces the brand.

offers self-esteem building tools for girls, moms, and mentors. Visitors that are interested in hosting a Dove Real Beauty Workshop can register to receive a free Facilitator Training Guide CD/DVD. The site also features inspirational stories about overcoming self-esteem challenges from girls, and viral films created by Dove. The Dove example indicates that there are many ways to bring the brand position to life. In this case, Dove developed an entire Web site dedicated to the brand's goal to widen the stereotypical definition of real beauty.

3. *Testing and early reads of products and communications.* On the Internet, new products can be introduced with minimal investment, and demand can be quickly determined. Additionally, with this information, insights can be gained as to who is purchasing what, thus helping to further tailor future decisions. Communications and advertising campaigns can also be introduced on the Web. Feedback from visitors and even copy tests can be quickly and accurately deployed so that changes can be made and the most effective message strategies and advertising tactics can be chosen before expanding into more expensive mainline media.

4. *Providing in-depth product and technical information.* Many businesses are using their Web sites to provide depth of content important to either the potential customer or the customer who has already made a purchase. TaylorMade Golf clubs puts information on their Web site about how to use the weights in their new sophisticated drivers. Lots of companies include in-depth warranty information on their sites. Detailed product handbooks are often displayed along with other technical information and advice. Business-to-business firms include product specifications and helpful ordering advice, and list the retail locations that sell their products.

Interactive Basics: Your Web Site

Your Web site can provide content far beyond what is affordable (or even practical) in the mass communication world. The Web site can also romance your brand and provide exciting content through on-site games, contests, chat rooms, and blogs. Finally, your Web site can be a marvelous selling tool. It can help you acquire and retain customers.

TIP

On your Web site, give your customers things that they can't get in the physical world and products and services they can't find elsewhere.

Your Web site should do a great job of communicating your brand positioning. Yes, it's a research and information tool and, yes, it's a selling tool. But if you don't also make it a branding tool, you're wasting a major opportunity to communicate who you are and why your brand is different.

Ann Taylor uses a simple, high-end feel to communicate with a more established female demographic looking for upper-end, fashion-oriented women's clothing. Urban Outfitters takes advantage of in-your-face colors and a less formal Web site layout to talk to a more urban, trendy, younger demographic (Figure 10.2).

TRAP

Don't ignore the feedback from your customers. They can be your most powerful selling tools.

Web sites that offer customer reviews have a competitive advantage over those that don't, according to the ForeSee Top 40 Online Retail Satisfaction Index. The company surveyed over 10,000 online visitors to one or more of the top 40 online retailers by revenue during the 2006 holiday shopping season. The study found that almost half the online shoppers that recalled seeing customer product reviews cited them as the primary factor in their hol-

Figure 10.2. Urban Outfitters Web site reinforces informal brand image

iday purchase decisions. The survey also found that customer product reviews drove satisfaction, are critical for first time buyers, and promote long-term loyalty to the brand.

Customer reviews provide you with a brutally honest check-up on how you're doing. They also act as a powerful selling tool. Customers often trust peer reviews over the company's word. Even negative reviews help legitimize good reviews in customers' minds. The review in Figure 10.3 was found on a national sporting goods company's Web site.

TIP

Customers want good information. Give it to them. Content is king on the Internet. Use the medium for its strengths—content-rich information, education and selection, and breadth of product.

Use your Web site to provide the best customer handbooks, reference guides, manuals, competitive analysis, and learning tools available in your industry. Educated customers are happy customers. The trust they gain on your site will be paid back with repeat purchases and word-of-mouth recommendations.

Let your customers buy when, where, and how they want to buy. In today's world, customers want to do research on, connect with, and buy your brand when and how they choose. That means they want options—from interacting with you while they are at work or at home, spending time in your retail outlet or office, or talking to your call center. To meet these demands, provide multiple channels of contact. If you aren't using the Internet to facilitate sales online, as a prepurchase tool, or to drive customers to your store, you're missing the fastest growing communication channel in today's marketplace.

Forrester Research estimated that almost $400 billion of store sales, or 16 percent of total retail sales, are *directly influenced* by the Web as consumers research products online and purchase them offline. It is estimated that this will reach $1 trillion in sales by 2012.

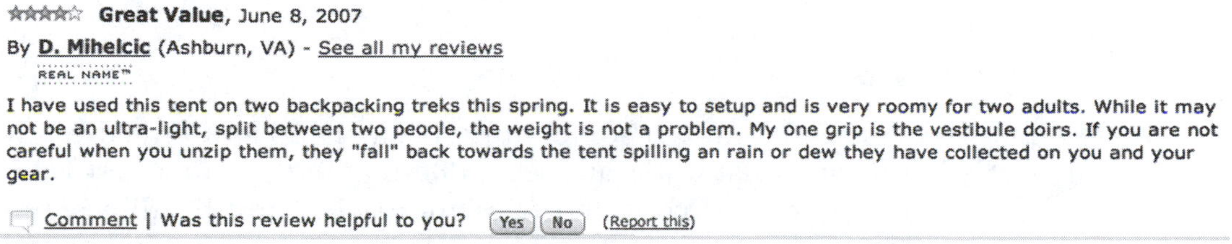

★★★★☆ **Great Value**, June 8, 2007
By **D. Mihelcic** (Ashburn, VA) - See all my reviews
REAL NAME™

I have used this tent on two backpacking treks this spring. It is easy to setup and is very roomy for two adults. While it may not be an ultra-light, split between two peoole, the weight is not a problem. My one grip is the vestibule doirs. If you are not careful when you unzip them, they "fall" back towards the tent spilling an rain or dew they have collected on you and your gear.

Comment | Was this review helpful to you? (Yes) (No) (Report this)

Figure 10.3. Honest customer feedback on a blog site

Slightly more than half of all shoppers have shopped some combination of Web, store, telephone, and catalog. Forrester also reports that 45 percent of all shoppers who searched online and then went to the store to purchase bought more than they intended, spending on average an incremental $154.

TIP

"Clicks and bricks" is often the strongest combination, because it lets consumers shop how and when they want, while still letting them physically touch and feel the product.

If you've got stores and an Internet site, connect the two together as much as possible. If you're a retailer, consider things like providing free in-store pick-up from orders on your Internet. Forrester reports that over 25 percent of the pick-ups will result in additional sales. If you're a business-to-business operation, use the Internet to solve technical questions and product information or to track orders for your customers.

Mercury Marine links interested consumers by zip code to the closest dealer. Additionally, they provide detailed product information and information on warranties and service contracts, which are most helpful before and after the sale.

Find ways to make the customer service function easier and quicker for your customers through your Web site and, in doing so, link the customer back to the store, office, rep network, or sales team.

Be sure not to confuse wants with needs. If you're in the retail business for climbing gear, recognize that your customers *want* to ice climb but they *need* the crampons to do it. You might research rock climbing online, then later search specifically for crampons. Talk about *wants* on your site. Then take care of *needs*.

A good example of this is www.patagonia.com. Patagonia is a company that sells what their customers want before they sell what they need. Through pictures, videos, and testimonials, Patagonia.com makes you really want to get out and surf, climb a mountain, or hike. Once they have you wanting it bad enough, guess where you'll turn to for surf wear or rock climbing gear?

TIP

Test, test, and test some more. It's a cheap and effective way to learn what works and what doesn't. Test product, test landing pages, test copy and sales approaches, test headlines, test visuals . . . test, test, test. Learn, learn, learn. Experiment and keep at it.

Interactive Basics: Internal Search and Navigation

Search gives your users the ability to find what they're looking for on your Web site. This includes finding specific brands, product categories, and information, and facilitating purchases.

Navigation is the science of moving users effortlessly (in their minds) from one section of your site to the next, in the user's own logical pattern. The easier it is to get around your Web site and to purchase (if your Web site is enabled for e-commerce), the longer people will stay on your site, the more "click-throughs" (pages visited) you'll have, which usually leads to more conversions (visitors who purchase).

TIP

Include your Web site address (also called the URL or uniform resource locator) in all your communications. Think of your URL as a part of your brand and a way for your customers to interact with your company. Include it in all your communications. Make it easy and intuitive for visitors to search and navigate your site.

Here are some considerations for both searches and navigation.

- *Name the categories and the products on your site in language the customer knows.* Use your customer's language and not your business's internal jargon. For example, if you're a shoe retailers, think about whether your customers refer to athletic shoes as tennis shoes, sneakers, or jogging shoes. It's their language that matters, not yours!

- *Tie your search programs together, if possible.* Don't do things that lead to dead-end searches. When people get to your site from search engines such as Google, make certain you put them on the correct path once they hit the site. For example, if a customer comes to your site looking for insurance, provide pathways that take them to life insurance, car insurance, home insurance, business insurance, etc. Think about the pathways that are critical to each of your products and provide easy avenues to get them there. People leave sites when they hit dead ends and can't easily move to the next level of interest in each category.

- *Monitor your failed searches.* When users get into your site but you don't get results (sales or length of stay), find out why. It can happen that users will come to your site for a certain word and your internal search engine returns no results. If this happens, you may need to rename a category.

Let's say you have a small shoe store and you notice that customers are coming to your site and searching for the brand "Ugg." If you don't carry Uggs, you'll *dead-end* their search. If you find this happening, take these potential customers to a page on your Web site that has Ugg-like shoes. Strategies like this improve your site's search efficiency and selling metrics.

Always help the customer make progress toward the information or products they are seeking. Find the dead ends and correct them.

Interactive Basics: Domain Names

Domain names, also referred to as *host* names, are memorable alphabetic names given to numeric Internet protocol addresses. By giving a Web site a memorable domain name such as www.yahoo.com, users are able to more effectively and efficiently search for and find the products and services they desire. Domain names have become one of the keys to a successful Web site for one obvious reason—your Web site is where you will direct all your potential customers. Owning a domain name has become so low cost (as low as $6.95 a year for registration), there is no reason your company shouldn't use it as a way to make a great first impression and hold a place in the mind of your customer. Once you own a domain name, it is yours to keep as long as you continue to renew your subscription. There are many companies that service domain name purchases. Among the most common are GoDaddy.com, and Networksolutions.com.

TIP

A short domain name will be more memorable. Own as many extensions on your domain name as you can. Pay for common misspellings and other names for your company.

Choosing a shorter domain name will make it easier to remember and may add credibility to your company. If you're choosing between two domain names: www.huntingsupplies.com and www.suppliesforpeoplewhohunt.com, pick the first (shorter, simpler name). Avoid domain names that could be confusing or misleading. If you're selling bicycles, make sure your domain name makes that clear. Avoid hyphens, as well as names that could be misspelled, as they may confuse and discourage potential customers. A website named www.Joe-bikeshop.com may be confused with www.Joebikeshop.com.

If you own wildsisters.org, you may want to own the .com, .net, and other extensions. Once you own them, you can redirect anyone who tries to go to those links to your .org Web site. If you type www.wikipedia.com into your address bar, you will automatically be redirected to the Wikipedia Web site at www.wikipedia.org. If you type www.chevy.com into your address bar, you will be redirected to www.chevrolet.com.

Intermediate Interactive: E-Mail Marketing

Besides its relatively inexpensive cost, one of the greatest advantages of e-mail marketing is that it delivers metrics that will allow you to measure your effectiveness, adjust your strategy, and achieve better results into the future. Examples of these measurable metrics are delivery rate, open rate, click-through rate, and conversion rate. These different metrics are explained later in this chapter. E-mail marketing, like your Web site, is also a comparatively inexpensive way to promote products and services, enhance and ensure customer service, build your brand, support promotions and product introductions in other media, and provide information to your customers.

E-mail is also very conducive to a "test and learn" environment. With e-mail, you know in a day how you performed with a certain offer, product, or e-mail content. Take this knowledge into other areas of your marketing.

Target your e-mails for increased effectiveness and response. Your e-mail list can come from users of your Internet site if you have a mechanism to capture their address. Often this is done by signing up Internet users and customers for a best customer or rewards club, or offering incentives such as rebates and discounts. Once you have their e-mail address, consider the following to help you get the most out of your e-mails:

- Segment by demographics or by expressed customer preferences.

- Segment users of certain products or product categories. Be relevant and provide information, content, and promotions for products you know are of interest to the segment.

- Segment users at certain times of the day and communicate with them just prior to when you know they are most likely to be on the Internet. This is most relevant for international customers.

- Personalize your e-mails whenever possible. Travelocity.com is a great example of knowing your customers. This Internet provider of travel customizes their e-mails based on where you live, where you travel, and the travel vendors you like to use (hotels, rental cars, and airlines). It's not uncommon to get a message talking about a great fare on travel from your hometown to your frequent destinations.

A common form of e-mail marketing that accomplishes this are e-zines (electronic magazines). An e-zine is a magazine or newsletter sent out periodically to a list of voluntary subscribers. E-zines stress the content aspect, concentrating primarily on information. Because your subscribers have given their consent to receive your newsletters, this is also a valuable tool for sending out promotions, ads, recommendations, and announcements.

TIP

E-mail marketing is an ongoing form of communication that provides information, creates excitement for your product, and connects your customers to your brand.

The two keys to a successful e-mail campaign are file growth and productivity.

- *File growth.* Create ways to continually expand your file or database of names. There are two ways to do this: retention of existing names and acquisition of new names. You can acquire new names through new member sign-ups, events, savings clubs, or other similar concepts. Offering perks or one-time savings is a great way to attract new names. Another is at your offline channel. Ask for e-mail addresses at the checkout stand.
- *Productivity.* Test your e-mail headlines, offers, images, time of day your e-mails are sent, and content against specific target segments. By understanding how different segments behave, such as which links they open and what they purchase, you will be able to cater more specifically to the needs of each segment and increase your productivity.

Pay close attention to the click-through rate (CTR) and conversion rate. The click-through rate is calculated by taking the number of clicks on links in the e-mail divided by the total number of e-mails sent out. This is basically how many people interact with your e-mails. The conversion rate is the number of people who take a desired action, such as purchasing a product or subscribing to a newsletter. These measures allow you to go past the *open rate* and down to the action level of your campaign.

A successful campaign will look not only at quantity, but also at quality. This means looking at the number of people that open your e-mail (quantity) but also the number who enter your site and complete a transaction. This conversion rate is another way of thinking about the return on investment (ROI) of your e-mail campaign.

TRAP

Don't just focus on one measure of effectiveness. The combination of visits, open rate, click-through rate, and conversion rate are all keys to determining how to improve your Internet performance.

The *open rate* (the number of e-mails opened, divided by the number of e-mails delivered), is a very important indicator, but should be analyzed with other metrics, such as conversion rate and click-through rate, to get a broader picture of your campaign effectiveness. You may find you have a high open rate but a low conversion rate. Tracking where the potential customer clicked could provide some answers. Do potential customers always dead-end (leave the site) at a specific product category or in certain parts of your site? If so, what are the possible causes? Can you confirm these through further consumer research?

TIP

Know the provisions of the "CAN-SPAM Act" (Controlling the Assault of Non-Solicited Pornography And Marketing Act of 2003).

The federal CAN-SPAM laws spell out the requirements for e-mail marketing. Each violation can result in a fine of up to $11,000. An example of a CAN-SPAM law is giving subscribers the ability to unsubscribe. Aside from it being the law, think about a time you tried to terminate a subscription to a newsletter but kept receiving it. It probably didn't leave you with a very good opinion of that Web site.

Subject lines and headings can make or break an e-mail marketing campaign. There are many ways to write a subject line or headline. Here are some common practices.

- *Use full names instead of e-mail names in headings.* If your name is Samuel Hall and your e-mail address is sghall@gmail.com, would you be more inclined to open an e-mail that read "Samuel Hall, great deals await you at yourfavoritecompany.com," or "sghall, great deals await you?" Keep in mind that it is not always possible to get a person's name. In these cases it may be better to use a generic salutation and to leave out "sghall."

- *Use your company name in the subject line and "from" line.* This will ensure credibility and let the receiver know that the e-mail is coming from a trusted source.

- *Use nondeceptive subject lines.* This is another provision in the CAN-SPAM laws. The subject line cannot mislead the recipient about the contents or subject matter of the message.

- *Test different subject lines.* You will get instant feedback on which styles work best and which do not. Use this information to your advantage and continue to try different messages and writing styles. Once you've found one that works, the more you use it, the more recognizable your e-mails will be to your recipients.

- *Write the subject line as if it is a newspaper headline.* This is your chance to really hook the reader and get them interested in what you are sending them. An unattractive, boring, or generic heading will likely not receive much attention.

- *Send it to yourself first.* Sending a trial e-mail to yourself, a family member or friend will provide instant feedback. What may seem like a good subject line at first may turn out to be flawed. This will reduce that uncertainty.

TIP

The use of e-mail messages to reinforce your Web content will significantly increase the productivity of your Internet site.

Use e-mails to reinforce content on your Web site, your in-store promotions, and your promotions in other media. E-mails can effectively support other mainline media. They can be used to remind customers that a specific sale is beginning or ending, that certain items are being previewed or are on sale, or that an event is occurring in your store or office.

A compelling offer can increase click-through and conversion rates. Be sure your offer is clearly stated within the first paragraph of the e-mail. Make the offer attractive and tell your customer why they should be interested and how they can benefit from your offer.

Avoid generic or sensationalized terms. Many spam filters will catch e-mails with headings such as "30-day guarantee" or "free trial." Exclamation points are also often a sure sign of spam. By avoiding these phrases you will increase your delivery rate, or the number of customers who see your e-mail, which will lead to a higher open rate. Services such as SpamCheck can be used to quickly score your e-mails, and can help guide you toward better word selection.

Confirm new subscribers. Before adding a potential subscriber to your e-mail list, make sure you confirm with them. This is referred to as "double opt-in" or "permission marketing," and is used to prevent someone from signing up an e-mail address without the owner's permission.

Follow the golden rule—pretend it is your name being added to a mailing list. Would you want your e-mail address to also be added to a second or a third list? How about a company trading for or buying your e-mail address? If you can't honestly answer "yes," then rethink doing it to your customers.

Hiring an expert can be a good investment. If you do not feel up to the challenge of writing subject headings or taking on your e-mail marketing efforts, hiring an expert can be an inexpensive way to ensure it is done right. Two major providers are Responsys and CheetahMail. Sometimes, hiring a whiz-kid college intern can be a fresh and useful addition to your Web efforts.

Intermediate Interactive: External Searches

An *external search* is what you use to make sure that customers who conduct a keyword search or query end up with your Web site name in the first page or two of their search results. There are two forms of external searches. One is *paid* and the other is *natural* or *unpaid*. Paying helps get you in the search game through sponsored links, but it won't guarantee a top spot on the first page of the results.

With natural search, search engines look at traffic to your site (generated from your URL and from affiliate partners who send traffic to your site) and relevancy (if the brand is yours, if you sell the brand, the number of times the word is used on your site, whether the word is in the page headline). These criteria determine your rank on the search engine's results.

Just because you have an Internet site doesn't mean that you'll get lots of hits each day. You have to play the search game very well. This can be expensive for those who aren't versed in how to effectively get people to their site. Be literate in both paid and natural search techniques or the time you spend building and populating your site with content will be wasted.

Intermediate Interactive: Paid External Searches

Paid search uses sponsored search engines, such as Google, to drive traffic to a Web site.

Paid Placement

Paid placement is a program by which listings are guaranteed to appear in the *sponsored links* section of the search results. With paid placement you can direct customers to one of many areas on your site: a homepage, brand page, search results, or even an individual product page. Paid placement programs are typically paid on either a cost-per-thousand pricing (CPM) basis or a cost-per-click (CPC) basis. With CPC, you bid on keywords or phrases and pay each time someone clicks on your link. The higher you bid, the higher your site will appear in the results. This type of keyword search is more expensive than paid inclusion advertising.

A word of caution—paid search isn't always as simple as "bid highest, be highest." There are many more factors involved, such as the increase in the value of relevance rankings. Multiple ads, rich content, and an in-depth Web site all count a lot in the rankings of your key words.

Choosing big players will lead to big results. In the near future, it is estimated that 90 percent of searches will use the big search engines such as Yahoo and Google. Smaller engines such as HotBot, MSN, and Dogpile will not get you the traffic you may desire. Choosing these big players will be more costly, but will ensure the traffic you need to optimize this service.

Monitor your keywords and phrases. After placing a bid, check to make sure you are appearing at or near the top of the list on your chosen search engines. You may find that you need to raise your bid, broaden or narrow your search parameters, or change the copy on your site.

TRAP

Don't try to be something you're not. Make sure your keywords tie to the content on your site and are as specific as possible. If you don't do this, you'll risk reprisals from search engines and attracting hits but ending up with lots of dead end searches on your site as customers find you aren't relevant.

Make your keywords relevant to the content of your Web site. If your keywords are not relevant to the contents of your site, you will be misleading possible customers. Additionally, many search engines, such as Yahoo, verify that the keywords for the sites they index actually match the content of those sites. Also, make sure your keywords are in your customers' language. Customers search using terms and phrases familiar to them, not your business lingo.

Generic keywords will empty your pockets. Choosing a generic keyword will boost your traffic but may not bring in sales. Keeping your keywords specific and targeted will reduce charges for unneeded click-throughs. Consider owning the keyword "landscaping" when all your company provides is simple gardening services. You may be channeling a lot of people into your site who are not interested in your product or service.

Buy your domain name and your brand name. People search for both www.famousfootwear.com and famous footwear. Owning both of these will ensure that they will find your site.

TIP

Target your paid search. The more you target, the higher the ROI will be on your paid search.

The more your ad or landing page matches the keyword intent, the better chance you'll have at a conversion or sale. But you can target even more specifically than with the keyword, the content of the landing page, or the content in the paid ad. The Internet also allows you to target geographically. If you're an architect, you can purchase "Illinois architect" to further target individuals looking for professional services within a specific geographic location.

There are four ways to target using keywords.

1. *Broad matches.* With broad matches, the search engines provide the broadest possible matches, including synonyms, plurals, and "close

matches." For example, you buy the keyword "athletic shoes." With a broad match, "athletic shoe," "athletic sneakers," and even "athletics" will show your ad or listing. This is the broadest form of targeting.

2. *Exact matches.* With exact matches, the query must exactly match your keyword. If you buy "Illinois architect" only both words together will list your ad.

3. *Phrase matches.* With phrase matches, your phrase must be included, but if the Internet user puts in other words in addition to the phrase match your ad will still appear.

4. *Negative keywords.* Negative keywords are those words that when they are included in the user's query the search engine will not list your ad, even if other keywords in the query match. For example, if you sell skis but you don't sell cross-country skis, you might list "backcountry" as a negative keyword. A high-end running shoe shop would exclude the word "sneaker," as no serious runner would ever put that into a keyword search.

Intermediate Interactive: Natural External Searches

Natural search includes a host of activities that can improve the ranking of your site by search engines. Tactics to increase your ranking by using natural search include embedding common words in your site that you know get searched. These words are either in the ad copy that customers see, or in the "metatags," which are Web site descriptions that only the search engines see. This increases the chance of your site coming up in keyword searches based on relevance.

TIP

Know the different tricks to effective natural search. Use the full combination to be effective. Don't just rely on one or two.

Use words customers know and use. Conduct keyword research to identify important words related to your products and your company's business. If you are a fashion store selling a parka, you will also want to include the simpler words such as "coat," in your description. Use the keywords in the copy throughout your site.

Make sure the title page tags (headlines) include keywords. Be cognizant of keywords that consumers use and put the words that directly tie to your site in all of your title page headlines. Provide compelling introductions to each page that will also get you credit for the content of the page during a natural search.

Don't put important keywords only in your Web site's graphics. Search engines use *Web crawlers*, which are computer programs that find key words on sites. Crawlers ignore graphics, so the result may be a dead end instead of a search at the next layer of detail. Make sure titles or captions are included in the text and not only in the graphics. That way, while the graphic will not be recognized, the caption will still be read. Additionally, whenever possible build navigation links to other sections of the site into the captions. This might help with relevancy, as an accumulation of pages and content helps show the site has robust information on the searched subject.

Make good use of metatags. Metatags contain information that describe the contents of the Web page. Metatags are not visible when the Web site is displayed to the user. They are not intended for users to see, but are created for search engine crawlers and browser software. Effective metatags, with words relevant to your business, help position your site higher in the results of a keyword search or query.

Maximize the number of *back links* to improve page rank. Back links are links from other sites to yours. Back links are also referred to as inbound links (IBL). Search engines use the quality and the quantity of back links to help determine search engine quality rankings.

Visit the webmaster guidelines page provided by the search engine. If you plan to use Google, visit their Webmaster Help Center to help Google find, index, and rank your site. You will also be provided with "Quality Guidelines" that will help you stay clear of practices that will get your Web site removed from the Google index.

Intermediate Interactive: Affiliates

Affiliates are typically other companies who will work to drive customers to your Web site. In most cases, you don't set up a direct relationship with an affiliate, but instead work through an affiliate aggregator like Commission Junction or Linkshare to develop your relationships. Affiliate marketing is unlike many of the other marketing channels available to marketers for one reason—you only pay for performance. Forrester Research reports that two-thirds of the top 400 online retailers run at least one affiliate program. Most run multiple programs. In a recent study by Forrester and Shop.org., 98 percent of all marketers participating in affiliate marketing rate it as *effective* or *very effective* in driving sales. Obviously, performance-based marketing gets results.

There are four major classifications of affiliates:

1. *Rewards affiliates:* These are companies that provide their customers rewards for dollars spent. The airlines would be a good example. United Airlines gives its customers miles when they purchase tickets. If you affiliate with United Airlines, a link to your company's Web site will

show up in a list of affiliate sponsors. When a United Airlines customer goes to your site, clicks, and purchases, the customer receives points for the purchase. Your company then pays United Airlines a commission for each hit or purchase depending upon how you've set up the affiliation. Another popular affiliate is Upromise. Upromise is a site set up to help people pay for their children's education. Families join Upromise and receive savings toward college when they shop and purchase at a large universe of top companies and products—from McDonald's to Exxon gasoline to Tide detergent.

2. *Deal affiliates or comparison shopping sites:* These sites consolidate information on all the best deals, sales, and provide coupons—in essence these sites consolidate and categorize all the deals, coupons, and sales by product categories. If you know you're going shopping for clothing, electronics, apparel, shoes, or sporting goods, you can go to these sites and find out who is offering what and at what price, in real time. These sites make money when a visitor goes to one of the advertisers and makes a purchase. Sometimes, the affiliate sweetens the offer by providing their customers part of the commissions they make from their advertisers. Sites like Fatwallet.com and Slickdeal.com provide not only deals but communication opportunities with other shoppers in forums and 24/7 answers to questions they have regarding products and the best deals.

   A clear example of a deal or comparison affiliate is www.kayak.com. Started by founders of Travelocity, Orbitz, and Expedia, this travel site searches for flights, hotels, cruises, etc., from over 120 different Web sites and gives you the best results.

3. *Search affiliates:* These help drive traffic to your site through both paid search on keywords and taking advantage of natural search to implant keywords throughout their site. Their reason for being is to land hits from keyword queries and then provide a path to your site—with a commission fee based on either the traffic they send or the purchases made.

4. *Incentive sites:* These sites use incentives to compel visitors to fill out leads or purchase items. A popular incentive site model is the well-known "free iPod"-type of Web site. You fill out a credit card application and you get a free iPod Shuffle or some similar incentive. Incentive sites are often used by Internet affiliates that offer advertisers placement in e-mails, banner ads, pop-ups and pop-unders, opt-in offers, lead generation, and trademark or keyword bidding. Incentives may come in the form of rebates, cash, products, points, etc. While incentivized clicks or traffic is the most notable incentive-based action, other forms such as incentivized registrations exist.

TRAP

The incentive affiliate has become known as questionable and borderline slimy. People often think they will be cheated and question their legitimacy. Use these at your own risk.

Make yourself attractive to your best affiliates. Score yourself against others using your affiliates. Affiliate partnerships require a lot of time—monitoring, answering questions, and providing advertising and copy. It's better to have a great relationship with a few good affiliates than poor relationships with many affiliates.

TIP

Choose affiliates that are consistent with your brand. Not all affiliates are scrupulous. Understand how an affiliate will promote your brand and what their strategy is to drive traffic. Create a contract identifying things you will allow and what should be avoided. Think of them as an extension of your brand.

Give your best affiliates lots of time so they continually put you up front in terms of on-site exposure. Provide them with your company strategies, offer them special deals that no one else can provide so that they remain viable with their customers. When you find a good affiliate that sends you business, work hard to keep them happy.

Intermediate Interactive: Banner Ads

A banner ad is a paid advertisement on a Web page. These ads are usually clickable, bringing consumers back to a Web site providing more information on the product or service in the ad. With Flash technology there is a lot you can do with your banner ads. It is possible to create full-length ads that play through your banner ad. Although it may not have the same effect as its TV counterpart, it is much cheaper. Consider the use of banner ads in larger Internet marketing campaigns when more proven forms of communication such as paid search, natural search, and e-mail marketing are in full motion.

Target, target, and target some more. Choosing which site will have your banner ad is a major part of targeting your audience. Choose sites that not only have high traffic, but have high levels of traffic from your target audience. A great example is on www.televisionwithoutpity.com. Networks will advertise new fall shows on the site to reach an audience that has already self-identified as being particularly interested in television and talking and reading about television shows.

Banner ads really are antithetical to the Internet experience. The Internet is a permissive medium not an intrusive one. Banner ads are really mainline media in a new media environment. When someone searches on a keyword, they want to find information. When a user goes to a URL or Internet address, they choose to be there. The Internet is filled with two-way communication opportunities. Banner ads are almost a throwback to the past. They violate the page and are not there at the choice or request of the Internet user. Keeping in mind the inherent problems with this type of communication on the Internet, you'll find that banner ads will work most effectively within content that is very relevant to what you're advertising in the banner ad. Click-through rates will be significantly higher when you follow this rule of thumb.

Banner ads are primarily for two purposes:

1. For generating clicks and attracting customers to your site.

2. For building brand awareness and image.

Tips for Generating Clicks and Attracting Customers to Your Site

Tell customers to click, and to click now, and make it interactive. Using words and phrases such as "click here," "click now," or "visit us now," tells your audience to take immediate action. You can also create a sense of urgency by using phrases such as "limited time only!" or "only while stocks last." This will give the viewer the idea that your site may be more important than the site they are currently viewing. Make sure these words and phrases stand out on the banner ad. They should really grab the viewer's eyes and demand attention. Making the viewer think they can interact with the banner ad is a great way to generate clicks.

Tips for Using Banner Ads for Branding

Banner ads can (and should) reinforce the image of the brand. This type of banner ad acts more as a billboard on the side of the road. The viewer certainly has the option to click on the ad, but the goal of these banner ads is more about building awareness than generating clicks. Flash media also offers the ability to create ads like those you would see on TV all within your banner ad. This can be a great way to catch a customer's attention and leave a positive impression.

TIP

Design the banner ad with a goal in mind. Make it consistent with your Web site, your overall company or product positioning, and your brand's communication tone and manner.

Understand that the use of banner ads is not only about branding your product but also about branding your Web site. The banner ad should give the viewer a good idea of what types of products or services are offered on your Web site. Google is a great example of a site that has really succeeded in this. When you think or talk about search engines, there is no doubt that you will mention Google. *Googling* has even become a verb for searching for something online.

Using the same colors and styles will help create a consistent brand for your product. If Coca-Cola created a banner ad, chances are it would have a good amount of red in it. Pepsi's ad, on the other hand, would have a lot of blue.

Finally, it is a good idea to give visitors somewhere to go. Although they may not click on your banner ad when they see it, providing them with your Web site or domain name increases the likelihood that they'll end up at your site sooner or later.

Advanced Interactive: Blogs and Social Networking

Social networking is drastically changing the marketing landscape. It is offering companies new and innovative ways to reach consumers and interact with them. Blogs of all kinds and sites such as MySpace and Facebook are now important affiliates for helping companies reach their marketing objectives.

Advanced Interactive: Blogs

A *blog*, which is a shortened term for Web log, is a frequently updated, user-generated Web site where users post entries that are displayed in reverse-chronological order. Blogs are often used to provide commentary about issues or specific genres such as politics or fashion. In the marketing world, blogs that are used to communicate a company's message or for other marketing, branding, or public relations purposes are called corporate blogs.

Within corporate blogs there are two main types; internal and external blogs. Internal corporate blogs are used as a great way to provoke discussion within your company and explore original ideas about which employees may otherwise remain silent. External corporate blogs' primary function is network-building. They serve as a way to persuade people to act in a certain way through discussions that effectively build relationships between key audiences. Businesses may also use this discussion as market research in an attempt to improve their business, conduct product testing, discuss marketing plans, etc.

Today there are over 40 million blogs, a number that is constantly growing. There are many services that exist to help you create a blog. Some examples are Blogger, msn spaces, and xanga.com. Once you decide to enter the *blogosphere*, decide whether a general public or a niche interest Web site would best suit your needs.

Blogs allow companies to target niche audiences. The ability to decide the audience for your blog allows you to reach very passionate audiences who often have very strong feelings and opinions regarding your product or service. If you are introducing a new service, this is a great way to reach these innovators and early adopters within your product or service area. For example, if your company produces electronics, you might consider conducting your blogging on engadget.com, which services the world of consumer electronics.

Nike connects with customers through providing a chance to blog on their Web site. Some Nike shoes come with a small sensor inside the shoes. The runner's iPod tracks the progress of the runner. Once home, the iPod is docked into the home computer and the details of the run are posted—including time, miles per hour, and description of the route, among other things. Other runners go online to discuss routes, training tips, and of course compare notes on shoes. The site has become a meeting place for runners, with many people coming to the site multiple times each week.

TIP

If you don't understand the social ethos of blogs, don't use them to promote your company. Blogs should be created by people who regularly use them, are familiar with the social norms, and understand the do's and don'ts of the medium. This is not the medium for the traditional copywriter.

Since blogs are user-created and unedited, you have little control over their content. If you get criticized, you are going to have to deal with it as if it were a newspaper article that cannot be taken from circulation. This is why many large corporations have been reluctant to enter this realm. If they do, they may need to have teams of folks constantly scanning the blogs for inappropriate content.

Don't create "fake" blogs. When creating a corporate blog, beware of making it seem like an advertising scheme instead of an interactive blog. Many companies have been criticized for creating blogs that contained fake comments. According to the audience, the main purpose of these "fake" blogs was simply to promote a product or service. Although some believe any publicity is good publicity, if your goal is to create a successful blog, this is not the way.

Keep your blog fresh and updated. Which blog are you more likely to check up on, one that is updated almost daily or one that is updated a couple of times a month? The more you keep your blog updated with new conversations, ideas, and information, the more likely your blog will have a large following.

Use your blog to tell a story. Engage readers of your blog with fascinating story-like entries. By captivating your audience you will have much more positive feedback and many more responses. Not to mention that this is a great way to communicate your company's strategy.

Track your blogs. Keep track of postings and try to get a feel for the major bloggers following your company. Once you feel you know who your most avid followers are, cater to them as if they are VIPs. Some of the bloggers writing about your company or even writing on your company site probably have their own blogs. A big-time blogger with a highly visited blog can attract upwards of 100,000 visitors a month, some a lot more. If a major blogger shows interest in your company, treat it as a major public relations project. Do not be afraid to contact these major players directly. They will often have their e-mail address readily available on their blog page; use this as a way to get a conversation going.

Don't ignore the small-time bloggers. Even bloggers who post only one comment can have an effect on your company. In 2004, a small blogger bragged that he could break a Kryptonite bike lock with a Bic pen. The post was picked up by some major bloggers and in no time it had reached *The New York Times*. The result? Kryptonite recalled all the locks and their brand name took a major hit.

Advanced Interactive: Social Networking Sites

Sites such as MySpace and Facebook have taken the online world by storm. If you are curious as to how big these sites are, consider this; if MySpace were a country, it would be the eleventh largest country in the world by population. Companies can use these sites to reach customers in new ways. Heavy users of these sites live online, play online, and purchase online. Their interactive nature is the key to using these sites as a platform for your Internet marketing efforts. Much has been written about the early stages of corporations using Facebook. Perhaps the best example to date is Target's successful Fall 2007 back-to-school campaign on Facebook, its "Dorm Survival Guide" page, which focused on designing your dorm room—of course using products available for purchase at Target.

There are over 200 social networking sites. Some cater to the general public, like MySpace and Xanga (a blogging community), while others cater to more niche interests. Linked In is a good example of catering to business professionals (www.linkedin.com). Some companies have even created their own social networks. www.MyCoke.com is a site created by Coca-Cola where users can socialize and earn points for Coca-Cola products. There are also a variety of services available through these sites. Youtube.com allows users to upload and share videos. Snapfish.com allows users to upload their digital photos and share them with friends and family and link them to social networking sites.

TIP

Social networking offers marketers new opportunities to reach consumers and offer the ability to efficiently target your marketing efforts.

The great thing about the Internet, and particularly about social network sites, is that if you can think of it, it can most likely be done. Whether you want to use these sites for banner ads, sponsor a contest, or launch a new product, it can be done. An example of this type of product/media launch is Fox using MySpace to debut its new show *Free Ride.* Another example is Toyota using MySpace to set up their own profile to promote their product and allow users to interact with the brand.

Facebook allows sponsors such as Apple Computer or Electronic Arts Gaming Group to create their own groups. Members of Facebook are then able to join the groups they are interested in. This can offer many advantages to a company, such as product and idea testing, generating feedback loops, or promoting new products.

Since many sites such as MySpace require personal information in order to sign up, it is possible to have your ads targeted at specific geographic regions, ages, and gender. Facebook currently allows advertisers to target users by selecting specific Facebook networks for their ads.

Now that you have the basics, the intermediate and the advanced tips and traps on interactive marketing, we'll end with one certainty. By the time this book is published, much of this will be standard practice, some will be out of practice, and there will be much that is new.

Internet Analytics

Appendix B provides a listing of suggested metrics to track customer activity and to help in creating tactics to improve the performance of your site.

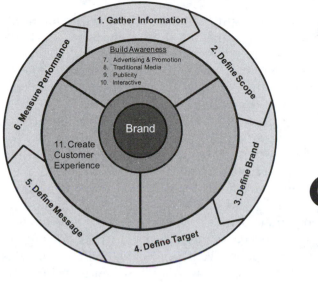

11

Creating the Customer Experience

We see our customers as invited guests to a party, and we are the hosts. It's our job every day to make every important aspect of the customer experience a little bit better.

—Jeff Bezos

How Do Customers Want To Feel?

When you order a book from Amazon.com, what is the experience like? Despite the fact that you are sitting in front of a computer, rather than in a coffee-scented retail environment, the experience is remarkably pleasant and easy. If you have been to Amazon before, they have remembered your login and password, so it is easy to get right to the books page. If you don't remember the exact title or author of the book, they help you identify it. Before you choose a book, you can read a bit about it—its jacket cover, a few pages, and reviews from others who have read the book. When you decide to purchase it, they have remembered all your address and credit card information, so you can easily check out. Before you do, they make a few suggestions of books you might also like to read, based on this and previous purchases. We have personally found these suggestions to be remarkably relevant, and have often ended up purchasing more than we initially intended. You can order a new book, or a used one to save some money. In just a few minutes you are done. You are sent an e-mail confirmation of your order to reassure you. And a few days later a smiling box appears with your book. Amazon.com does a remarkable job of making the purchasing experience pleasant and easy.

There are certain important moments of truth when you experience a brand: when you first learn about the brand, when you purchase the brand, and when you use the brand. Good marketers understand these moments of truth and do whatever they can to make you feel good about all three.

To highlight the increasing importance of the experience of a brand, Joe Pine and James Gilmore demonstrate with a powerful metaphor in their book, *The Experience Economy*: the birthday party. There was a time when most parents would purchase the raw ingredients for a birthday cake: eggs, milk, sugar, flour, powdered sugar, vanilla and butter. All told, it probably cost no more than $2 to prepare. But then Betty Crocker came along and made it much easier for us to prepare the cake. We just added some milk and eggs to the mix and opened up a can of frosting. We happily paid a bit more for this value-added convenience. But there was a way to add even more value. The local baker and grocery store figured out that if they baked and decorated the cakes, consumers would buy them. For the ease of picking up a cake at the local store, we paid even more, about $10. Finally, Chucky Cheese came along and offered a complete party experience: cake, pizza, and entertainment. For this, some parents happily pay $150. What has happened is that an experience has been added to the offering, for which we will gladly pay. Adding an enjoyable experience to the product added significant value.

Every marketer needs to consider the experiences a brand's customers have at these moments of truth.

TIP

Today, it is no longer enough to just sell products. Consumers expect a brand experience.

Recently, McKinsey & Company did a study on the effects of a good experience versus a bad one at a brand's moment of truth in banking. They identified two groups of the bank's customers: those who had experienced a positive "moment of truth" and those who had experienced a negative one. Among the group who experienced a positive moment of truth, 58 percent said that they increased the value of the products they purchased at the bank such as checking accounts, savings accounts, CDs, and loans. Among those who experienced a negative moment of truth, 23 percent bought a product at another bank, 15 percent switched banks, 20 percent stopped using the product, and 14 percent decreased the value of the products they purchased at the bank. Only 28 percent did nothing. Brand experiences matter because experiences are emotional, and emotions drive behavior.

While there are many ways of creating the brand experience, we will address a few critical ones in this book. In marketing, it is common to talk about consumer "touchpoints." These are all the places a customer may come in contact with your brand. They could include your Web site, your product, your customer service department, even the receptionist at your office.

Identify the key touchpoints of your brand experience. Take a moment to consider the key touchpoints for your brand. If you made some improvements to the key ones, would it have an effect on sales? A.G. Laffley, CEO of the marketing giant Procter & Gamble, recently stated, "It's not about being at all the touchpoints. It's about being at the right touchpoints when the consumer is open to it."

The Product or Service Experience

There is perhaps no more important element of your marketing mix than the quality and performance of your product or service. When you build awareness for your brand, you build your customer's expectations. It is a key moment of truth when they experience your product or service.

Psychologists talk about the concept of "imprinting." Imprinting happens when a child experiences something new for the first time. Especially if the first exposure is emotional (frightening, joyful, funny, etc.), that first exposure can leave an impression that lasts for a lifetime.

A customer's first exposure to your product or service is critical. Try asking someone who grew up in France to try root beer. In the United States, root beer can be found at any soda fountain or restaurant. In France, they cringe at the flavor, because it reminds them of a certain cough syrup they had as a child—and who would want to drink a cough syrup–flavored soda?

One bad experience can turn a customer off to your brand forever. That first exposure to the product or service is critical. Nothing will put you out of business faster than implementing a sampling program for an inferior product.

What is your customers' first experience and what are you doing to imprint your brand in their memory? Whether it's the flawless service, the consistent words that the sales associates uses, the music the customers hears and associates with your product, the extra-special box, the postpurchase experience, or the uniqueness of the product experience itself—as the saying goes, you never get a second chance to make a first impression.

TIP

If you are providing samples of your product, make sure the product delivers on expectations. The packaging can do more than just protect your product. It can enhance the usage experience.

The value of a product is in the total value it offers your customer. For example, Burger King has always sold French fries. But recently, they significantly enhanced the customer value of this product experience by offering it in a cardboard container designed to fit in a car's cup holder.

In 2006, Vonage ran lots of commercials about their VoIP Internet phone service. They were funny commercials about people doing dumb things. The implication was that it was a dumb thing to continue paying for traditional phone service, when you could get the same service at a much lower cost through Vonage. The authors recently tried their offer and ordered the necessary router and hookup. When it arrived, we tried to install it, but it didn't work, so we got on the customer service line with Vonage. After spending an hour and a half (on a beautiful Saturday afternoon) with four different marginally helpful customer service reps, Vonage decided that the router must have been damaged in transit. We were so frustrated with their poor customer service, we sent the damaged router back and vowed never to use Vonage again. It didn't surprise us to later learn that their business model was sinking fast.

Customer service is part of the product experience. Apparently, we're not the only ones frustrated with their service. The following is from an actual blog about VoIP communications.

> Vonnage [sic] Sucks! Yea . . . I Said It!
>
> Ok . . . now that I got that out in the open. LOL No real secret if you've followed any of the posts in this blog on broadband phones. I . . . don't . . . like . . . Vonnage. Why? Here's just 2 easy reasons . . . they've built their business on a massive marketing campaign, not quality of their service . . . and they cost more than everybody else but act like they don't. Yea, snappy commercial jingle but "where's the beef"?
>
> Plus . . . they're being very secretive about their real future. Don't be fooled by that supposed recent huge influx of investor capital and their impending IPO. Their real future (according to Russell Shaw of ZDNet.com) is to sell themselves off to one of the Telecom big players for a big score as soon as they're attractive enough. Now what do you think will happen THEN? Price goes up more . . . and quality goes down more.

In the year after Vonage Holdings went public, their stock price fell from $15 to $3. Make sure your brand experience delivers on customer expectations!

The Retail Experience

Have you ever found yourself walking out of a store with far more than you expected to purchase—and feeling good about it? You probably didn't even notice all the subtle things going on in the retail environment that helped you feel good about parting with your hard-earned dollars and walking out with an armful of expensive merchandise.

One of the most important elements of strong marketing these days, whether it is in a bricks and mortar store or online, is the experience you can create for your customer around their interactions with your brand. Even if you are not a retailer, it is important to understand the critical role the retail environment plays.

Most of this you may never notice as a shopper, unless you are really paying attention. When you walk into a store, what do you notice? Is the music loud and full of energy or is it soft and soothing—or is there no music at all? Are the fixtures contemporary, old-fashioned, in bold colors, or do they fade into the store so that you hardly notice them? What about the floors—are they inlaid wood, carpet, tile, or cement, noticeable or hardly noticeable? Is the store fully staffed or is it set up for self-service? Has the store incorporated technology into its merchandising, is it visually-oriented, are the senses overloaded or hardly awakened?

Why does a hot, creative ad agency's office look different from the old-line respectable lawyer's office? What would you think if your architect's office looked like your insurance broker's office?

If you are the manufacturer of a grocery product, to some extent you are at the mercy of the grocer—but not completely. For example, you can choose to market your product through traditional grocery channels, like Kroger, or limit distribution to health food stores, like Whole Foods. Different images come to mind. Those images halo your product.

There are even small things you can do to affect the selling environment of your product when your product has two distribution steps; i.e., selling to one business that ultimately sells to your final end-user. Even when you are not responsible for the selling environment, you can influence it. You're in charge of your packaging, which has a huge influence on how the customer feels about your product. You can work with the grocer or retailer to create special point-of-sale devices to enhance your product and the selling environment around it. You can even work with the retailer to create in-store events that help connect your product to your target market.

Our discussion of the retail experience alone could take up an entire book. It includes things like the store layout, the overall ambience, the traffic flow, music, visuals, staffing interactions, mirrors, transition zones—all the pieces of the store or office that help reinforce your brand and positively connect the customer to it. This chapter touches on some of the most important aspects of the retail experience.

Good marketers take time on a regular basis to stand in front of a busy retail store and just watch the traffic flow of customers. Paco Underhill, who wrote the book, *Why We Buy: The Science of Shopping*, spends more time doing that than just about anyone. He and his firm Envirosell spend their time studying shoppers and videotaping hours and hours of customer behaviors as they shop different retail environments. They have learned a lot about *how* consumers shop. For example, they have explored questions such as:

- How many people turn right or left or go straight when entering the store?
- How much time do people spend in each section, their total time in the store, and the conversion rate of shoppers to buyers?
- How many people read the information on packages or at the point of sale before buying?
- When a parent shops with a child, what effect does that child have on the shopping experience?
- When are shoppers most likely to buy and when aren't they?
- How do people move through a store?
- What things tend to engage shoppers and which things do they avoid?
- How do customers interact with the signage in a store?
- Do they understand the pricing scenarios?
- Are they attracted by the displays?

TIP

Understanding how and when your customer interacts with your product in the shopping environment is key to improving your conversion rate (percent of customers who actually purchase) and units per purchase.

They have also discovered barriers to good merchandising. These are often simple things that have to do with consumer behavior. For example, Paco talks about the "butt brush" factor: shoppers, and especially women, don't like being brushed or touched from behind. This typically happens when aisles are too narrow as they bend down to self-select merchandise. They'll move away from sections of the store or merchandise to avoid this unpleasant experience.

It is also critical to understand *when* your customer shops. In his book, Paco reports that only 4 percent of browsers purchase computers on a Saturday before 12 noon versus 21 percent after 5 p.m. That's a powerful finding for a computer retailer. Staffing decisions, sales objectives, incentive programs, space planning, marketing, and security should all be affected by this finding.

At Famous Footwear, we understand that our customers have a hierarchy of places where they like to spend their time in our stores. The vast majority of shoppers turn right when entering our stores and then go back to the clearance area. We've taken this traffic pattern and turned it to our advantage; we put the newer higher-margin women's shoes directly into that initial traffic pattern and we improved the shopping experience in our clearance area.

TIP

The amount of time a customer spends in your store is one of the most critical factors that determines how much they will buy. What are you doing to help keep your customer in the store?

The retail environment affects how long a customer stays in your store or office. Here are a few things to think about when considering how you might increase the length of their stay.

1. Are you in the business of simply selling goods or are you providing entertainment for your customers? *Retailing* is defined as the sale of goods and services to consumers. We believe that more businesses should think in terms of "entertailing," or entertaining consumers in an environment where there are goods and services for sale. The marketplace is quickly moving beyond the mere selling of goods and services. Consumers are demanding to be entertained (for example, Rainforest Café, The Apple Store, and REI) and to experience the merchandise and the brands with which they are connected emotionally.

2. Have you merchandised your store 360 degrees? Each store has a "pathway" that most customers take. You should find out, through observing traffic, the percentage of customers that go left, go right, make it to each department or merchandise category, shop the accessories, and make it all the way to the back of your store. In doing this, you'll get ideas where best to create displays and points of interest to help keep customers engaged. Most retail stores merchandise with only a front to back view in mind. However, many stores do a good job of getting customers all the way through the store to the back but then they have no points of interest as the customers make their way back to the front for the actual purchase. Merchandise front to back and back to front. Kohl's department store has solved this potential problem by creating a circle around the store; most customers get on the "track" and go in a complete circle around the store, and they are presented with merchandise and displays on both sides of the track.

3. The front quadrant of a store is typically the hot spot. This is often the first destination for the customer and the area most likely to be shopped. Take advantage of the front quadrant to display the latest

trends and the newest merchandise. Spend time and money here to create relevant displays that change often and stay fresh. Work to keep the customers in this area longer. After all, it should be the most interesting spot in your store. Finally, leverage this area to lead customers to other areas of the store. Create interest here and highlight other experiences they can discover in your shopping environment. Do this through signage, cross-ruff or cross-promotional coupons providing incentives to shop other sections of the store, and clear traffic pathways that make it easy to move to the next section.

TRAP

Understand the stopping power and the promoting power of your in-store communication. You need both.

Signage and in-store communication work on two different levels. Communication and displays both stop shoppers and promote shopping. If you're undertaking a research project to judge the effectiveness of your in-store communication, you should measure both.

There are many things you can do to help with stopping power. Consider some of the following:

1. Signage and displays are really about good communication. Create a message strategy for your signs and displays just as you would for an ad. Signs are simply great billboards, so all of the rules apply. The headline should grab and you shouldn't use more than five to six words in the major portion of the communication block. Black type on a light background almost always reads better than reversed type. Make sure your signs are consistent with your brand. If your brand is about "fun," make sure even the restroom signs are done in a manner that is consistent with the larger communication of the brand—make them fun. Caribou Coffee shops do a great job of consistently giving a feeling of the north woods throughout their retail environments (Figure 11.1).

2. When creating signage and merchandise displays, consider the sightline of the customers. If the customer can't see it, the signage won't be effective. We've seen lots of observation studies that point out signage that simply can't be easily read or seen. One of Target's strengths is how easy they make it for shoppers to see and read the signs and prices. America is aging. Make signs easy to read.

3. Too many signs create "visual pollution" and actually reduce readership of all signs. Make a few big statements.

Figure 11.1. Caribou Coffee's signage and displays reinforce the feeling of the north woods.

4. Signs in major traffic pathways should have copy that only takes a few seconds to read. Signage in waiting areas, on the other hand, should be longer and more complex since customers are standing still.

After you've stopped them, make sure your communication promotes shopping.

1. Please touch! Make interaction with your product and brand easy. Encourage touching, involvement, interaction, and first-hand experience.

2. Make sure you are relevant. Work to determine the most relevant promotions, sales, ways to communicate attributes, services that are most meaningful to your customers, hours of operation, and just about anything else that might matter to your customer. If you're going to communicate in-store, the most important thing you can do to promote actual shopping is to have information that matters and displays that create want. Most people have all they need. You need to create desire.

TRAP

Just as white space is important in an ad, it's important in your store, on your packaging, and in your office.

White space creates impact. It draws attention to things you'd like to highlight. Make good use of it. There are certain situations in which retailers create crowded looks because that's the concept of their brand (the flea-market approach). But in most cases, beware of clutter. It makes everything look the same.

The notion of the "landing pad" is a well-known retail concept that also applies to your offices. It's the area just inside the door. Good retail science shows the importance of providing customers a space from which to preview the store and orient themselves. A good landing space provides a platform to see the whole retail brand, determine the layout, and view highlighted areas in the first quadrant of the store.

TRAP

Self-service does not mean ignoring the customer. Contact with customers almost always increases the sales rate.

Don't waste your customers' time. If you do, they won't come back. Make them wait, confuse them with an overload of signage, staff your store with people that can't provide answers to questions about the product or installation, and you'll quickly lose customers. Today's consumer is just like you and me. They have less time today than they did yesterday. Time has become one of our most valued commodities. Don't waste it for your customers.

The key is to figure out the proper contact for your store or service organization. There's a big difference between a self-service environment and a full-service one. In a self-service environment, people don't expect a heavy sales pitch. Research has shown that people are very comfortable in a self-service environment and in many cases prefer it. That doesn't mean they want to be ignored. Usually, simply acknowledging customers leads to a more productive shopping experience. Finding the right way to interact leads to a significantly more productive shopping experience. At Famous Footwear, we added a free home-delivery shipping program that allows our sales associates to help customers who can't find their size in the shoe they want. The result—over 3 percent of sales now come through this form of employee contact. The program lets the staff be heroes ("Really, you can get me this shoe!?") and helps connect the customer and store personnel in a meaningful way.

All the *senses* matter—they communicate to the customer. Take advantage of this through sound, smell, and taste. However, in the end, each of the senses you use needs to be consistent with the mood you're trying to create and consistent with your brand.

PacSun and Abercrombie & Fitch connect with their teenage target by connecting them with their music. Women are connected to Bath & Body Works through fragrant flavorful indulgences. In department stores, this is done in the fragrance area through sampling. Whole Foods and Trader Joe's create connections through in-store sampling programs that use the taste buds to connect customers to the products they sell and to their retail brands.

Lighting and mirrors can add to sales. The brightness and coloring affect how customers perceive and interact with your brand. The Lighting Research Center in Troy, New York, reported that colored LEDs (light-emitting diodes) not only cut costs but also attracted more customer attention in window displays. This was determined via a series of mall intercepts after customers were exposed to the window displays with and without the colored lighting.

A rule of thumb is that light is good and natural light is better. People like to see what they're buying. In the fall of 1999, a landmark study entitled *Skylighting and Retail Sales* was done for Pacific Gas and Electric Company by the Hesuhung Mahone Group. They studied a chain of 108 retail stores: two-thirds had skylights and one-third did not. All of the other factors were basically the same. Multivariate statistical analysis allowed for the control of other variables besides lighting. The results showed that the skylights positively and significantly contributed to higher sales. In fact, they accounted for *40 percent higher sales* with a significance of 99 percent. The skylights' effect on sales was second only to the number of hours the stores were open.

Mirrors in a retail setting let people look at what they have on. It's a simple truth that mirrors lead to sales. It's also a fact that most retailers don't provide enough of them. If you listen to what customers say when asked about retail shopping environments, they almost always ask for more mirrors. Mirrors also get shoppers to slow down or stop, ultimately leading too more time in your store.

But let's go beyond the traditional retail setting. Lands' End figured out the power of mirrors while selling on the Web. The catalog retailer knows the power of letting customers see what they are trying on and they knew that this added to the conversion and sales rate.

If you visit the Lands' End Web site, you'll notice they have two levels of "mirrors" to help with conversion. The first level includes information that makes them an authority and helps a customer feel confident that he or she is making the right decision. Let's look at swimsuits, for many women perhaps one of their hardest-to-fit apparel purchases. A suit can make a woman look great . . . or not so great. Lands' End makes it easy and mitigates some of the risk of a bad decision. The customer can virtually try the suit on a model she selects (who looks like she thinks she does) using Lands' End's trademarked Virtual Model. The service allows customers a virtual mirror. They can try swim suits or any other clothing on a figure that can move in a 360 degree circle, so they can see the front, sides, and back.

Mirrors are important, but hopefully this section convinces you that it's not mirrors but the idea of letting people experience the product and see it as part of them that is the real motivator.

Marketing Planning Model

12
Managing Customer Relationships

There is only one boss: the customer, and he (or she) can fire everyone in the company from the chairman and down, simply by spending their money somewhere else.
—Sam Walton

The final step on your marketing planning journey is to make sure that you establish an ongoing relationship with your customer. Marketing has evolved from a one-way communication path to an ongoing dialogue of which the customer is in control. The top marketing companies have discovered that the lifetime value of a customer is far more important than making a quick sale.

The best way to actively manage the lifetime value of your hard-earned customers is to develop the practice of a customer relationship management program. Acquisition of new customers, without the ability to retain and grow their profitable involvement with your organization, will never result in a successful business platform.

Customer Relationship Marketing (CRM)

Customer relationship management, or CRM, has finally arrived. After years of promise and misuse, the discipline has become the backbone and heavy lifter for many businesses who have learned three things:

1. Obtaining new customers is very expensive.

2. The existing customer who stays with you is your most profitable customer.

3. There is a lot to be learned from examining the profile and habits of your best customers.

CRM can be defined as much by what it *is not* as by what it *is*.
CRM *is not*:

- A computer program to data mine and capture customer data.
- A method to change customer behavior.
- A coupon and promotion program.

CRM is a long-term program designed to help you understand your customer. Its purpose is to profitably improve the connection and the relationship you have with your customers and the relationship your customers have with your company. CRM is about understanding and insights. Successful CRM programs require:

- Understanding your target market customers and looking at common behavior segments that exist within your target market. Each segment, while having the common characteristic of the overall target market, should clearly exhibit meaningful differences from other segments within your broader target market.
- Understanding what your customers purchase and determining which customer segments look to your company for which sets of products.
- Understanding what your customers want from you beyond merely your products. Analyze service, frequency of purchase, and the emotional reasons they have for buying from you.
- Understanding how your customers react to various communications, product offerings, promotions, and events.

Effective CRM comes from the top of the organization. Before you start a CRM program or if you want to improve an existing program, make sure you have support from the top of the organization. There are three main reasons for this:

1. CRM is truly a multifunctional program. It is not owned by the marketing department, the product department, or those providing service to the customers. It cuts across all aspects and all departments of the organization that affect the customer.

2. CRM requires a significant investment in software and technology. You have to be able to capture purchase data at the point of sale, then

store, query, and disseminate the data into actionable reports. There has to be a financial commitment to the CRM program.

3. CRM results in a test and learn environment. Therefore, decisions about both strategic and tactical direction are continually required to take advantage of what is learned. Without top-down involvement, the CRM program gets stalled—it ends up simply grinding out data and findings only to have them stored and ignored. In this situation, those involved eventually realize that their work is irrelevant, and eventually the entire CRM program gets marginalized.

 TRAP

Lack of up-front planning results in a failed CRM program. Carefully plan the structure of your database and CRM program so that it benefits the entire organization.

Here are a few considerations to avoid this trap:

- CRM is most effective when the program receives senior management support. Particularly important is for the organization to gain consensus around what is most important goal. Is the goal to drive top-line sales, build the brand image, drive margin dollars or margin percent, increase retention of customers, gain new customers, or something else?

- Get all stakeholders involved in the initial design of your CRM program and in the ongoing plans and development.

- Do you plan to have a rewards program that's based on points and thus reward purchases every so often, or will your reward program involve every purchase for customers that qualify?

- Do the rewards have to do with monetary incentives, an experience with your company, or both?

- Do you also plan to use your CRM program to communicate your positioning with product previews and events?

- What's the intended scope of your program—do you eventually want 90 percent of the customers to be part of your CRM program or just the best of the best and thus a small percentage of your very heavy spenders?

- What types of information do you want to capture regarding your CRM customers and how do you foresee sharing and using this information throughout the company?

Solve clearly defined problems with specific objectives. Don't try to change an entire business. Define problems that need to be solved. Examples of common problems can include:

- *Very little customer loyalty.* Customers exhibit a propensity to shop multiple channels, competitors, or they have a large consideration set when purchasing your product.
- *Small share of the customer wallet.* Your brand is only getting a small percentage of a customer's purchases in the category.
- *High trial rate but lack of retention.* Or, you discover that retention is difficult with first-year customers but after two or more years customers become extremely productive.
- *Single purchases.* Customers purchase only one product category across your product line.

Create clearly defined objectives that can be monitored and that, when accomplished, will clearly move toward solving the problems identified. Consider the following as realistic thought starters for your objectives:

- Improve retention of first-year customers.
- Get customers who haven't purchased over a period of time back to being purchasers.
- Increase the number of times a customer purchases or uses your services.
- Get customers to use other products and services within your organization.

TRAP

CRM is not a mass program, it's a best-customer program. If you run it like a mass media program you'll lose money and effectiveness. CRM is a one-to-one medium. It's about two-way communication that says to the customer—"they know me and want to find out more about me."

Mass advertising tries to make every person who sees the ad happy and feel good about your company. CRM is about evaluating customer potential and spending more on those that mean more to you. CRM is all about best customers. For your CRM program to succeed, you need to identify clusters or segments of your customer base that will respond to very targeted communications at greater rates than a mass audience. If you try to turn your CRM into a mass marketing program you'll find that your expenses outpace your revenues. The cost per thousand reached in most mass market vehicles is a fraction of the cost of meaningfully interacting with a CRM customer via mail or events. The one place in which the cost is extremely low is Internet contact. However, the time involved in really learning and dissecting segment needs and wants and then translating these into products and communication programs is very extensive.

At Famous Footwear, we have one target market segment called the *Fashion Value Mom* (a woman 35 to 54 years of age, with children, who loves shoe purchasing, is a spontaneous shoe purchaser, and purchases for the whole family but buys more shoes for herself—especially dress and casual shoes). This Fashion Value target market segment accounts for 32 percent of all purchasers and 46 percent of all pairs of shoes purchased. Additionally, we have nine segments under this target market segment based on purchase behavior. For example, 25 percent of the target market falls into the "whole store" segment—those that make purchases across the whole store. There's a "kids" segment that primarily uses Famous Footwear for kids' purchases, a "fashion athletic" segment, a "performance athletic" segment, a "fashion dress" segment, and a "casual" segment, along with three other segments.

These segments form the foundation of our CRM program and we use this segmentation to merchandise and communicate to these segments on a regular basis. These segments make up our best customer program and account for 25 percent of all total customers and 50 percent of the organization's sales. Each segment receives different communication based on the products they purchase, the offers to which they are most responsive, and the receptivity they have to move into other categories of purchases.

It's easy to get lost in the details of CRM.

- Don't oversegment. In the extreme, you could end up with each individual customer being a segment. Oversegmentation is how CRM programs end up with negative return on investment. Find meaningful segments but remember, the software today makes it easy to create segments that are so small and have such minute differences that segmentation simply becomes an academic exercise.

- Invest in the segments that yield the biggest dividends. For example, at Famous Footwear, three of the nine CRM segments make up 60 percent of the CRM database and also have the largest lifetime value. It is on these three segments that Famous Footwear spends the majority of its CRM dollars.

- Don't overtest. You can test, test, and test some more without really making any fundamental changes. And don't get stuck in analysis paralysis, in which you test the same ideas again and again without any decisions on improvements. It's an easy discipline in which to simply "do tasks" and appear to be very, very busy (and in need of more and more money for implementation).

CRM is all about measurement, but measurement is important only if you test what is meaningful and act on what you learn. There are a million things you could be testing. Test those with the largest potential to significantly improve your business. CRM technology and software allows for the ongoing testing of ideas. The trick is to understand the metrics that are most important to the organization and then to measure against these.

The following are examples of things a company might prioritize for testing.

- What's the incremental response time from new members receiving their first contact?
- What combinations of incentive and product inserts and timing (inserts combined with incentives or as a follow-up) work best to promote redemption and total response?
- What recovery (getting back lapsed customers) incentive works best and is most profitable?
- What creative formats work best?
- What segments are the best predictors of incremental response to various incentives?
- What pure product pieces drive the best response for different segments?

You should have a yearly test plan. Don't just randomly test things, but concentrate on an area and do enough tests so that you can find the right answers and move on to other areas. Remember, you can only test one variable at a time, so you often have to run multiple tests of similar ideas to separate out what works best.

Make sure to hold out control populations that allow you to statistically prove that the tests perform below, the same, or above the control or the group of customers that did not receive the test communication.

The biggest challenge is to act upon what the tests show you. We'd suggest a standing meeting of cross-functional leaders who meet to review test results and determine the action to be taken in the future.

TIP

Recency, frequency, and monetary (RFM) measurements drive the first phase of CRM monitoring.

The first phase of measurement against your segments should be the recency of purchase, the frequency of purchase, and the amount of purchase. Customers that have purchased most recently from you, with the greatest amount spent, and with the most frequent purchases will typically be your most profitable customers.

Utilizing models beyond RFM can also drive a higher response from customers. With models, the key is that while they are statistically significant it is often difficult to isolate the attributes which make the biggest difference. For example, you could build a model for a particular communication piece that will help predict customers who are most likely to respond. Attributes that could affect response might be competition, the distance the customer lives from the store, or the competitive nature of the store's trading area. Certainly, all of these attributes combined into a model will make the results more robust than simply using RFM. However, it's nearly impossible to build a model that considers every attribute. Often you must plug in one attribute and analyze its potential impact with respect to the model. Models are certainly effective; however, there are several examples of the simple RFM methodology beating a complex statistical model in overall response rates and profitable response rates.

TIP

Measure the overall success of your program toward increasing the lifetime value of your best customers.

The long-term success of your CRM program should be measured by the lifetime value that your best customers provide your company. You typically figure this by taking the average lifetime of a customer as a purchaser and calculating the income stream that can be expected over that time period.

TRAP

Don't just go by the numbers. How you communicate is just as important as knowing the behavior of each customer and each customer segment. Spend time understanding both the rational and emotional sides of CRM.

It's one thing to understand the numbers—how frequently a segment purchases, the average dollar amount per purchase, the average retention rate, the number of purchases during sale events, and so on. However, it's also important to determine *how* you should talk to each customer segment.

Develop a customer profile or snapshot of each customer. What are their shopping habits (when and what do they buy)? What are the purchase motivators (what do customers in each segment look for in the shopping experience)? What are the attributes that are important to them? What are the key messages and language you should use? What are the key times of the year during which it is most important to communicate with each segment?

These snapshots will serve as valuable bridges from your customers to the creative teams responsible for developing your communications to your most valuable customers.

CRM is changing the way we communicate with our customers—from one-way communication to two-way communication. Today, more than at any other time in business, there is the opportunity to change the relationship dynamics from one-way communication from the company to all potential consumers to two-way communication between the company and its customers. Customers are willing to provide information about their product use, their attitudes, their expectations of the communication you provide, and how they want to be communicated with—in return for more targeted, more relevant, and better-timed communications. This also leads to the elimination of unwanted, generic, and poorly timed communications.

With the advent of chat rooms, blogs, and community networks on the Internet, companies have a new channel available through which their best customers can become ambassadors for the company. Through CRM, companies can identify their best customers and provide them with information that is more relevant. The CRM program of the future will make it easy for these customers to connect with other customers and potential customers by leveraging technology to encourage positive information sharing.

Finally, here is a personal testimonial from one of the authors of what CRM can do to help an organization.

Five years ago at Famous Footwear, the CRM program was in the red because it was viewed as a direct mail program instead of a best-customer program. We took the following steps to turn it into a best-customer program.

- We tightened the criteria for membership in our database or rewards program and made it a point-based program, which encouraged an ongoing relationship with Famous Footwear to receive actual monetary incentives. In our minds, the program is for heavy users and is structured to gain more of them and to reward this section of our customer base for their loyalty.

- We created a mix of reward (for quantity of purchase) and nonreward communication (product previews, events in the store, birthday cards).

- We installed the technology and software that was necessary for us to ask questions, implement tests, and get the results.

- We monitored key metrics (retention, purchase amounts, purchase frequency, margin dollars, purchase on-discount versus off-discount) across new members, first-year members, and 2+ members (members that had been with us more than two years).

- We created nine segments based on purchasing patterns. These segments ran across the new, first-year, and 2+ members. Examples of segments at Famous Footwear include: all family (purchase across all shoe categories), kids (primarily use the store for kids purchases), women's fashion, women's fashion athletic, women's performance athletic, men's all store, men's athletic, women's casual, and junior/fashion forward.

The results:

- Our Rewards member sales went from 17 percent of our total business to a planned 50 percent in 2007.

- Contribution or incremental margin dollars less marketing costs soared over 500 percent.

- Active Rewards members grew over 200 percent, so that 25 percent of the customers now account for 50 percent of the sales. More importantly, the database customers spend $10 more per transaction and have twice the transactions of nonmembers. The average spent per customer is more than double that of noncustomers. And 75 percent of the purchases are nondiscount purchases.

- Multichannel customers are growing. The customer who purchases both on the Internet and in the Famous Footwear stores significantly outperforms the Rewards customers, who significantly outperform the non-Rewards customer.

- The retention of first, second, and third-year Rewards members continues to increase.

- The organization has embraced CRM, and the field staff are the leaders in recognizing the importance of the program to their individual market and store performance. The support of the field has led to unparalleled success at obtaining new members at the point of sale. Additionally, the customer behavior information is also used in real estate decisions and to help the merchandise department classify customer groups, as Famous Footwear begins to localize buying decisions.

Marketing Planning Model

13

Innovation— Your Marketing Engine

Every business has two principal functions—marketing and innovation.

—Peter Drucker

You may have heard the story about the frog in the cooking pot. It's said that if you put a frog in a pot of boiling water it will jump out, but if you put a frog in lukewarm water and slowly heat it up to boiling, the frog will not sense the gradual temperature change and will stay in the pot and cook. Now we have never tried this, but it is a great analogy for marketing your business. Your marketing environment is constantly changing, and organizations must recognize those changes to stay relevant (and profitable). Innovation is the engine that drives your marketing and your business.

At Wal-Mart (and many other large retailers), every six months they reset their "planogram" for most product categories. This means they systematically look through every stock keeping unit (SKU) and rank them by sales. To keep merchandise on their shelves that is desired by their shoppers, they drop the bottom 20 percent of SKUs in the category and add new items. In certain categories, the turnover rate is even greater than this. Wal-Mart needs to keep its product offering fresh because this is what their customer wants and this is what drives their sales. The implications of this for companies selling products to Wal-Mart are huge—Innovate or die.

What Is Innovation?

Innovation is not just coming up with new ideas. Many good ideas never get to market. Some are ahead of their time. Some get to market without the proper level of awareness-building marketing support. A good idea without good execution is ultimately not worth anything because it never creates value. The simplest definition of innovation that we have heard is:

Innovation = creativity applied to create value.

This means having a good new product or service idea and the skills and ability to develop it, get it to market, and generate profitable sales from it.

Innovation Requires Both Creativity and Discipline

When we think of creative and innovative companies like Apple and Lego, we imagine creative gurus and wacky offices with employees playing Frisbee. While there is an element of this in most innovative companies, there is also an intense discipline and a process for innovation that guides which new products and services make it to market and which ones are killed.

TIP

Generate lots of ideas. Make it a discipline to devote time to generate innovative ideas for all areas of your business on a regular basis.

According to Robert Cooper, new product consultant and author of *Winning at New Products,* only about one in 11 ideas makes it successfully to market in most big companies. Innovative thinking should become part of your routine so that you have plenty of good ideas to choose from. If you don't, you will find yourself in the unfortunate position of wasting time and effort to develop mediocre ideas. You may also find yourself needing to launch some of these ideas—which becomes a very costly strategy when the ideas fail.

TRAP

Spreading your innovation resources across too many ideas. All of your marketing resources are precious. Bad ideas can take as much of your time and effort as good ideas.

Every idea requires resources to develop. The best companies are good at killing the bad ideas early so that they can focus their precious resources on the best ideas. The very best companies generate *lots* of ideas in strategic areas at the "fuzzy front end," and then ruthlessly sort through them with consumer concept tests and feasibility tests.

Innovation Strategies

What is your company really good at? What insight do you have about your customer that the competition does not? How can you use this to your advantage to innovate? What emotion should your new products and services deliver? These are all questions that you should ask yourself as you develop your innovation strategy. If you do, you will be ahead of many companies, who don't even consider these questions.

Successful businesses have a strategy and a process for innovating. The innovation strategy guides choices about the markets in which to innovate, which kinds of products or services should be developed, and which consumer needs should be addressed.

TIP

With new products, keep one foot in the familiar. If the idea appears too unfamiliar to your target, they may reject it because they are uncomfortable with it.

Many product launches are unsuccessful because the product is simply ahead of its time. Most consumers need a familiar frame of reference to feel good about trying new products. If your product is very innovative, find a way to talk about it that makes it seem more familiar.

Was the Pontiac Aztek an SUV or a funny-shaped sedan? Nobody really knew. Launched in 2000, *Mad Magazine* called it "the ugliest car in American history," and it was discontinued in 2005 (Figure 13.1).

When we think of innovation, we often think of products like Apple's iPod or Motorola's RAZR phone. These companies have been very successful at developing and launching home-run products. What many people miss, however, is that they also launched many modest upgrades and extensions

Figure 13.1. The Pontiac Aztek. Was it a sedan or an SUV? Photo provided courtesy of General Motors.

to these blockbusters that kept the offering fresh and generated incremental revenue. Within these companies, there is a portfolio of product innovations being considered and being developed for launch.

TIP

Develop a portfolio of innovative ideas from the incremental to the spectacular. Some companies make the mistake of going only for the home runs. Others only for the singles. You need both.

The singles are the ones that keep your company moving forward while you are looking for the home run. However, a portfolio filled with only line-extensions is a recipe for long-term brand confusion.

Putting all your bets on a home run is a precarious strategy because home-runs are difficult and risky to successfully develop. Customers need the singles too.

Different products and services may play different roles for a company. Apple has sold a lot of iPods, but their popularity has also helped drive incremental sales of their computers. At U-Haul, the boxes they sell you when you rent a truck might look like an afterthought, but they actually represent the most profitable part of U-Haul's business. Dodge didn't sell a lot of Vipers, but it helped put it back on the map as a brand that could generate excitement.

TIP

Define the roles you want your product and service innovations to play within your portfolio.

Not all launches are designed to boost profits. Some may be image builders and others may be volume generators.

As a whole, your new product and service launches need to meet your profit goals, but you should have the flexibility to launch individual outliers if they address a strategic business or brand need.

What are customers looking for? What unmet needs do they have? How do they use your existing products and services? What do they think of your innovation ideas? With the Internet, it has never been easier to get feedback on your innovations. There are online panels, blogs, and concept testing services. It is better to get your customers' input early and often, than to spend the resources to launch an idea that is destined to fail.

TIP

Keep your customer involved in the innovation process, from the insight gathering and concept generation through prototyping and in-use testing.

The best companies are always checking in with consumers. Whether it is ethnographic or anthropologic studies to gain insights on consumer needs and behaviors, focus groups or in-depth interviews to check concepts, or quantitative tests to check the appeal of prototypes or advertising messages, these companies involve the customer in every step of the innovation process.

TRAP

Relying on the president's opinion rather than on solid research and a disciplined innovation process.

In some companies, product and service innovation is guided by the whims of a strong-minded president. While some are brilliant (e.g., Steve Jobs) most research shows that company presidents are not very good at picking new product winners.

Cost reductions are also a legitimate place on which to focus some of your innovation. Cost savings projects are low-risk and go directly to the bottom line. Just be mindful of how you do it. Let's say you are a fan of Taco Bell. If they discovered a way to lower the price of a burrito by 10 percent, this would be a good thing, as long as they didn't sacrifice taste or quality. If you are looking for ways to innovate in cost, from a consumer's perspective it is better for you to find the costs in the process than in the product's quality.

Innovation Processes

Think of product development as a steeplechase horse race, with each of the horses trying to get over the hurdles to the finish line. Some will fall along the way. It is a game of probabilities. Your goal is to place your bets (resources) on the horses (ideas) that get over the hurdles (development milestones) and have the greatest likelihood of finishing the race and being successful. The best way to ensure winners is to make sure that you have a lot of "horses" (good ideas) at the starting gate.

It is fairly standard practice at most large companies to have a "stage gate model" to manage their product innovation. This is simply a process of tracking products through various stages of development to see if they are meeting their financial and performance "hurdles," and making decisions at these milestones to either kill or further support the development of the product. The first stage of this process is often called the "fuzzy front end," because this is where insights are gathered and all the wacky ideas get thrown into the innovation funnel.

TIP

The source of good ideas may be outside your company. To get new ideas, look at as many different sources as you can.

There was at time when companies felt they needed to do all their own R&D and develop all their own ideas internally. This has changed dramatically. Procter & Gamble now seeks to get at least half of its new product ideas from *outside* of the company.

Outside vendors, suppliers, customers, outside inventors, your ad agency, and design shops can all be good sources of ideas.

TIP

A concept is the cheapest form of prototyping.

The first milestone might be a strategy and feasibility check on an idea. Does it fit into where you are trying to go with the brand? Is it something your company could successfully manufacture, license, and market? At the end of this stage, you may concept test the idea by putting it in front of consumers for feedback.

It is much cheaper to understand the appeal of your concept than to spend money to develop a new product that has an unappealing concept. It is important to screen out ideas early that have little consumer appeal.

Even if you don't have the resources to do a quantitative test on your concepts, take the time to write a headline and some descriptive copy for your idea and show it to some potential customers. Do they understand it? Do they find it appealing?

The next phase is often called development, in which prototypes are developed and tested. If successful, the idea may move into production and launch. In these final phases, the big investments are made, as machines are ramped up for production and the product is launched onto the market.

As you move through the feasibility, development, and launch stages of innovation, try to stay true to the idea embodied in the winning concept. It is very easy to get off track along the way. R&D may tell you they can't quite deliver the benefit described in the concept. The ad agency may tell you they have a completely different idea for how to sell the concept. If you have identified a winning idea in the concept testing, stick to it.

Innovation is not just the job of your marketing and R&D departments. Innovation is not just about new products and services. Finding new, more efficient ways to manufacture a product or deliver a service is an important part of every business. You can and should innovate in your selling strategies, your brand communication, and the way you go to market. The market is always changing and your business needs to stay relevant.

14

A Final Word on Marketing Your Business

Marketing should be fun. For us, it has always been the most interesting part of business. It is at the intersection of psychology, mythology, storytelling, anthropology, science, and commerce. Good marketers are usually curious, interesting, empathetic people, who try to keep up with the latest trends. Good marketers have a sense of the timeless patterns of human psychology and behaviors as well as a knack for seeing those patterns applied in fresh new ways that bring new relevance to them as the culture and the market changes.

As anyone who has teenaged kids knows, the best way to get them to do something is usually not to tell them what to do, but to help them discover for themselves why they want to do it. Consumers are no different. To be successful, you need to artfully engage them and help them feel something about your brand, which starts with understanding how you feel about your brand or company.

There are any number of things you could tell your customer about your brand and your product. But marketing is the art and science of sacrifice. It is the art of asking just the right questions, listening to and observing customers very carefully, and communicating in a fresh and authentic voice. It is having the insight and discipline to keep your brands relevant and differentiated.

Every business for which we have worked has had a noble, inspirational aspect to the product or brand. The good marketer is the one who is able do identify this aspect—to discover the most authentic and compelling story of the brand and to celebrate it in a compelling way. We wish you much success and hope the tips and traps provided in this book help to guide your marketing and grow your business.

Appendix A

A Consumer Behavior Framework

Awareness

Consumers become aware of a product through a number of communication sources, such as advertising, the Internet, public relations efforts, and not least of all, from friends and neighbors or business associates who have experience with the product.

Attitude Formation

Once consumers become aware of a business or product, they start paying attention to communication and other learning cues, such as casual conversation with friends, mass media information, Internet searches, etc., and they form an attitude about the product. At this stage, the consumer starts to come to a conclusion as to how the product compares to others—is it more fashionable, a better value, or do they connect to it in some emotional fashion (value, attitude, lifestyle)? In other words, a brand identity starts to form in the consumer's mind.

Trial and Repeat

After using or consuming the product or service, the consumer decides whether to purchase the product again. This repeat purchase decision is based on whether the consumer's perceptions and attitudes toward the product were met after actually experiencing the product. Depending upon the decision at this point, the consumer shows some degree of loyalty toward the product—on one extreme, becoming brand loyal to the point of excluding all other choices, and on the other extreme, becoming extremely non-brand loyal and never purchasing the product again.

Not all products are purchased in this manner. There are many situations in which the consumer is purchasing a product with which they have little ego involvement and the product isn't that important to them. Examples might be chewing gum or basic cleaning materials, and many other product categories in which there is low ego involvement and thus a low risk involved in simply trying the product. In these cases, the product is purchased first, then awareness is built, the product is tried, the consumer forms an attitude about the product and decides whether or not to purchase it again.

The whole point of developing unique brand positioning is so that you are able to meaningfully differentiate your product and provide a unique emotional connection to a segment of purchasers. The job of marketing is to create product value with consumers. Product value is achieved through following the awareness/attitude/behavior model and affecting each part of it. Therefore, the following model provides us with a key understanding as to what needs to be accomplished in terms of communication and marketing objectives. Let's see how.

Basic Consumer Purchase Model

How It Works

The basic model (Figure A.1) works as follows. You have a target market that is a certain size. The target market would be made up of customers and non-customers that fit your target market profile as established in the target mar-

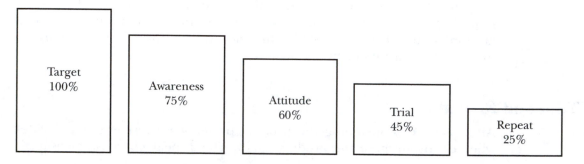

Figure A.1. Basic Consumer Purchase Model

ket chapter of this book (Chapter 4). Your total target market might be 100,000 people or businesses. Only a certain percentage of the total target market will be aware of your product (75 percent); and of those that are aware, only a certain percentage will have a positive attitude (60 percent); and of those that have a positive attitude, only a certain percentage will try your product (45 percent); and of those, only a certain percentage will repeat the experience (25 percent).

Information You Need to Capture

The following information should be captured for each of the categories in the consumer behavior model. Most of this will be captured through consumer research. If your company cannot afford the $15,000 to $75,000 it will take to conduct this research, you can either provide best estimates to the questions below, which should allow you to be in the ballpark, or you can use secondary sources such as MRI (Marketing Research Insight) and SMRB (Simmons Market Research Bureau), which provide similar information for many consumer brands. Finally, many trade magazines, trade journals, and trade associations provide much of this information for business-to-business company categories and products.

Target Market Information

How many total customers and noncustomers fit your target market profile developed in the target market chapter (Chapter 4)?

1. List the number of customers and non customers you have that fit in your target market profile.
2. Under this target market profile, are there a number of individual segments? If so, list the number of customers and non customers that fit into each segment.

Note: An example of a consumer *target market* might be men, aged 25 to 54 years, who were athletes growing up, love sports, and who want to stay active. *Segments* might include breakouts by geography or by the different types of sports in which they participated (team, individual, or even specific sports), etc.

In the business-to-business area, an example would be a *target market* of businesses in the $5 million to $1 billion range. *Segments* could include breakouts by SIC code, such as retail, finance, and so on, and even smaller breakouts that include segments within finance, such as banks or insurance companies. Additionally, the segments might include geographic breakouts, customer tenure, how the product is used, other buying habits, or decision-making processes (bid, committee, etc).

Awareness

Of the total customers and noncustomers who fit your target market profile, what percentage of people are aware of your company or product?

1. What is the *unaided awareness* of your company and business relative to your key competition? Unaided awareness comes from asking the open-ended question, "What companies or products come to mind when you are looking for . . . ?" (e.g., legal services, shoes, fast food, business supplies). Unaided awareness is the most realistic measure of whether your target market profile knows you and how strongly your brand is known among both your target market profile and other consumers in your brand's category.

2. What is the *first-mention awareness* of your brand? This measures the percentage of respondents who mention your brand first. First-mention or top-of-mind is an even stronger measure of your company's awareness and provides you with a directional sense of your company's market share. You typically won't be first in market share if you are fifth in first-mention unaided awareness.

3. What is the *aided awareness* of your company or products? Aided awareness is just that, it's an unaided awareness question followed up with probes. A question might be, "What fast food restaurants are you familiar with?" The respondent might answer, McDonald's, Burger King, and Subway. These are all *unaided* responses and the respondent most likely frequents these establishments the most, with McDonald's being their favorite. Now if the respondent was asked, "Are you familiar with Arby's?" that would constitute an *aided* response. A "yes" answer means they know of Arby's, so the fast food restaurant is at least in the considered set. However, chances are, it is still not favored, because Arby's was not included in the respondent's unaided responses.

TRAP

Don't get fooled by aided awareness.

Aided awareness is by far the weakest measure of awareness. Aided awareness either means you are known but not liked or barely known and not considered in the person's chosen set.

TIP

Make sure to compare results of awareness ranking to that of your competition.

Knowing how you rank relative to other competitors provides a realistic measure of how much you need to improve awareness in order to be competition.

Attributes

TRAP

Measure attributes that are critical to your positioning.

If you don't measure the important attributes, you will be judging attitudes on things that don't apply to how you've chosen to brand your company or its products. Go back to your brand positioning to make sure you are measuring relevant attributes and decision factors.

1. What are the critical decision factors or attributes that determine whether the target market uses your business or buys your products? How do you rate on these relative to the competition?
2. Of those that are aware of your company or product, what percentage have positive attitudes toward your company or product?

TIP

Make sure to compare results of attribute ranking to that of your competition.

Knowing how you rank relative to other competitors provides a realistic measure of how much you need to improve in order to be competitive.

Trial

Of those that have positive attitudes, what percent have tried your product?

1. How many individual people or businesses have used your company and/or products?
2. What is the average number and amount of sales per customer? How many times does the average person shop or purchase from your company and what is the average dollar amount?

TIP

Make sure to compare the trial figures for your company to that of your competitors and the industry.

This is especially helpful when you start establishing objectives. For example, if your figures are significantly above that of the industry, there is less incentive to significantly increase trial rates. This type of information helps you set realistic objectives.

Note: You will need to translate this into what's pertinent to your business. If you are a retailer, you'll want to track things like total number of transactions, average number of transactions per customer, average sales per transaction, and average items sold per transaction.

If you work for a service firm, you'll want to track things like number of visits, average sales per visit, and number of services used per visit.

Repeat Behavior

Of those that try your product, what percentage tries it again?

This measures the loyalty of your customers. Keep track of repeat purchase rates or the percentage of customers that purchase more than once in any given period of time (one year, two years, three years).

TIP

Make sure to compare the repeat trial figures for your company to that of your competitors and the industry.

As with the above example, this is especially helpful when you start establishing objectives. For example, if you are significantly below the industry in repeat purchase, there is more of an incentive around significantly increasing repeat purchase rates.

How to Use the Model

The following scenarios provide a first look into how the basic consumer model works and the decision making power it will give you throughout your marketing process.

Scenario: Low Awareness Problem

In Figure A.2, the company has low awareness. However, of those that are aware of the company or its products, a high percentage have favorable attitudes toward the company on the attributes critical to its brand positioning. Additionally, of those that have favorable attitudes, there is a high degree of both trial and retrial. In summary, customers like the product and try it again. This company needs to focus on building awareness.

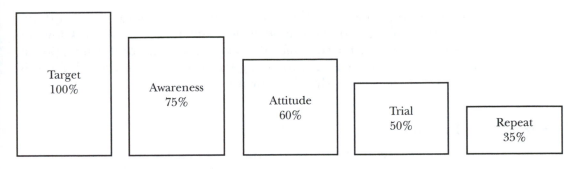

Figure A.2. Low Awareness Problem

Scenario: Poor Perceptions

In Figure A.3, the company suffers from poor perceptions or attitudes toward its products. The firm has plenty of awareness. But of those that are aware, only a small percentage have positive attitudes. However, after this drop, things get better. There is a large percentage of people with positive attitudes who try the products and then provide a repeat purchase. Something has happened that created what appears to be a wrong perception regarding the company and its products. This might lead to communication objectives that call for an increase in positive attitudes around things most critical to the brand positioning of the company. This might then lead to communication strategies to improve perception and, eventually, marketing strategies dealing with improved product, improved customer service, or other improvements to back up the claims made in the company's communications.

TIP
Perception equals reality in the world of marketing.

Figure A.3. Poor Perceptions or Attitudes

Perceptions aren't always fair but they are real. If your target market thinks you are performing poorly on some critical attribute, even if you know this can't be true, then you have to face the fact that you are performing poorly. Until you take bold measures to change and to communicate differently, you will be perceived poorly—fairly or not.

Scenario: Poor Product

In Figure A.4, the product is clearly the problem. There is high awareness. However, of those that are aware, only a small percentage has a positive attitude. Further, very few of those who have a positive attitude and who try the product, try it again. Clearly, there is a need to improve the product or the service customers are getting after purchasing the product. This would lead to marketing objectives dealing with increases in retention and gaining new trial. Strategies to accomplish this would include improvements in product, changes in customer service, and then communication of these changes.

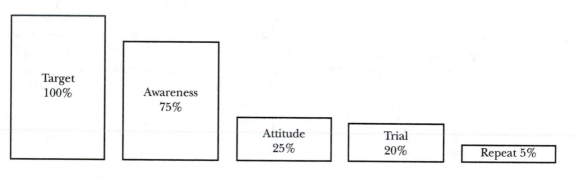

Figure A.4. Poor Product Problem

Appendix B
Internet Analytics

Internet Analytics

The Internet is unique in its ability to track and measure consumer activity. A good option for smaller businesses is Google Analytics. Other providers are Omniture and ThinkMetrics. They will give you some measurements for free as a starting point. Some of the analytic data commonly available from the Internet include:

- *Sales:* total, by product, by page; or by segment.
- *Top 10 items and brands sold on-line:* total and by segment.
- *Sales by gender:* total and by segment.
- *Multichannel shopping* (purchase at two or more channels—store, Internet, catalog, telephone): total and by segment.
- *Sales by geographic segments:* top performance by DMA (designated market area or television viewing area), by city, by SMSA (Standard Metropolitan Statistical Area, geographic areas designated by the U.S. Census Bureau).
- *Total hits or visits:* total and by segment.
- *Number of new visitors and repeat visitors:* total and by segment.
- *Conversion* (percent of visitors that purchase): total and by segment.
- *Site traffic* (where people are coming from and going to on the site, hits on any given product or content section): total and by segment.
- *Click stream or path analysis:* where people look on your site.

- *Sales by Internet marketing program:* direct to site, natural search, e-mail, affiliates, paid search, comparison shopping.

- *E-mail file size and segment size:* sales, number of purchases, conversion, purchase by product type, by total number of e-mail messages, and by segment within those messages.

- *Retention rates:* total and by segment.

- *Web-to-store features:* visits to store locator and visits to store, total and by segment. (Note: This assumes your site has a store locator that can provide real-time inventory analysis to let the Internet customer know if the product is available in the nearest store location. It also assumes that the retailer has a rewards program to track customer purchases in the store.)

- *Units per transaction:* total and for segments.

- *Sales, returns, net sales, orders, average order size, margin, and operating profit:* total and by segment.

- *Top performing products each month:* total and by segment.

- *Top performing brands each month:* total and by segment.

- *Top search engine links:* by visit, total and by segment.

- *Top internal searches:* total and by segment.

- *Top failed searches:* total and by segment.

- *E-mail visits and sales:* total and by segment.

- *Total customer reviews:* favorable versus unfavorable by category.

- *Return on investment (ROI):* benefit gained in return for the cost of your ad campaign. Your click-through rate and your conversion rate, combined with your advertising costs, can help you assess the ROI of your campaign. It is also helpful to assess the ROI of your paid search in comparison to natural search.

Some of the above, in terms of tracking user pathways and click-throughs, require tracking mechanisms. Examples include tokens, beacons, and cookies. Tokens are used to count unique users. Beacons track the visitor's actions, and cookies identify return visitors and help track their actions once they are on your site.

Index

Note: Page numbers in *italics* refer to figures or tables.

About the Authors

Scott Cooper

Scott is President of Marketing Engine Group, a marketing planning firm. He has a unique background, having worked in all three sides of marketing planning—corporate, agency, and teaching/writing. He was Senior Vice President of Corporate Marketing and Branding for Brown Shoe Corporation, a $2.7B leader in wholesale and retail footwear brands and Senior Vice President of Marketing for Famous Footwear, a family footwear retailer with over 1,000 locations. Prior to that, Scott was President of The Hiebing Group, a brand marketing firm with national clients such as AAA, Mercury Marine, Coors Beer, and Culligan. Scott has written three other best-selling books on marketing planning published by McGraw Hill. He has taught at the University of Wisconsin Business School and he has led seminar workshops for businesses of all sizes. He has a BS in economics from the University of Wisconsin and an MBA from Miami University, Oxford, Ohio. Contact Scott at www.marketingenginegroup.com.

Fritz Grutzner

Fritz has over 20 years of experience helping companies build winning brand strategies in the U.S. and abroad. He is President of Brandgarten, a brand strategy firm that helps companies discover their true brand story and tell it in a compelling way. Before founding Brandgarten, Fritz was Vice President of Marketing for Johnson & Johnson's baby products. As a brand strategist, Fritz has been using his understanding of the emotional power of brands and storytelling to grow brands like Snap-on Tools, Oscar Mayer, Snapper, KI, Eli Lilly, and Heatilator, and for non-profit organizations like The Wilderness Society and The Wisconsin Historical Society. He has an MA in Germanic Philology from the University of Wisconsin and an MBA from the Thunderbird School of Global Management. He can be reached at www.brandgarten.com.

Birk Cooper

Birk has a BA in consumer sciences from the University of Wisconsin in Madison. As a project manager at Brandgarten, he has worked with such groups as Plastic Ingenuity, Conney Safety, The Wisconsin Historical Society, Anchor Wall Systems, and the Wisconsin Entrepreneur's Network.